MAKING CAREER DECISIONS THAT COUNT

A PRACTICAL GUIDE

MAKING CAREER DECISIONS THAT COUNT

A PRACTICAL GUIDE

Darrell Anthony Luzzo

AUBURN UNIVERSITY

Gorsuch Scarisbrick, Publishers

SCOTTSDALE, ARIZONA

Publisher:	Gay L. Pauley
Editor:	Shari Jo Hehr
Developmental Editor:	Katie E. Bradford
Production Manager:	Mary B. Cullen
Cover Design:	Don Giannatti
Typesetting:	John & Rhonda Wincek/Aerocraft

Gorsuch Scarisbrick, Publishers
8233 Via Paseo del Norte, Suite F-400
Scottsdale, AZ 85258

10 9 8 7 6 5 4 3 2 1

ISBN 0-89787-827-2

Printed in the United States of America.

Brief Contents

For a complete table of contents, see page vii.

Contents

Preface

Career decision making is a lifelong process. The experiences we have during childhood and adolescence help us develop attitudes about the world of work and form the basis of some of our earliest career aspirations. As we enter adulthood, our skills and values become increasingly important as we narrow our interests down to the two or three careers that we're most likely to pursue. It's at that point that a clear understanding of the career decision-making process becomes critical. As just about every career counselor will attest, the most fulfilling and rewarding career decisions are made by those who understand what the career decision-making process is all about.

Making Career Decisions That Count: A Practical Guide is written specifically to help college students learn more about the multifaceted nature of career decision making as they engage in various career exploration and planning activities. Case studies of actual students and career decision makers are integrated throughout the book to illustrate important concepts and clarify the complexity of the career decision-making process. Interesting and informative chapter exercises provide students with hands-on opportunities to put their newfound knowledge into practice. Students will appreciate the user-friendly tone of the book, and instructors will benefit from the logical organization of the chapters.

Chapter 1, "Understanding the World of Work," introduces students to Dr. Anne Roe's system for classifying careers and encourages students to keep up with labor trends and job projections as they learn more about career decision-making strategies. Chapter 2, "The Developmental Process of Making Career Decisions," presents Donald Super's theory of career development and provides students with detailed examples of the various stages of the career decision-making process. Students learn firsthand that making an effective career decision requires an increased awareness of self-concept.

In Chapter 3, "Assessing Your Personality, Interests, Abilities, and Experiences," and Chapter 4, "Recognizing the Importance of Your Values," students complete several exercises designed to help them learn more about their personalities, interests, skills, and values. Then, in Chapter 5, "Integrating Information About Yourself," students evaluate their career-related self-concepts and make some initial career decisions based on the results of the assessments completed in Chapters 3 and 4. As Chapter 5 concludes, students are encouraged to narrow their list of career options to the four or five that seem most worthy of continued exploration.

Chapter 6, "Methods of Career Exploration," introduces students to multiple resources that can be used for gathering career-related information. Included in the chapter are descriptions of the *Occupational Outlook Handbook*, the *Dictionary of Occupational Titles*, the use of the internet in career decision making, and over 20 other sources of information that students will find useful. The chapter also provides students with helpful hints and strategies regarding informational interviewing, job shadowing, and the importance of part-time and volunteer work experiences as valuable methods of career exploration.

Chapter 7, "Identifying and Overcoming the Barriers," helps students think constructively about the role of barriers in the career decision-making process. After learning about the differences between real and perceived, internal and external barriers, students complete a series of exercises to assist them in identifying career-related barriers and developing effective strategies for overcoming them.

With an increased awareness of their self-concepts and a clearer understanding of the career decision-making process, students narrow their career options down even further in Chapter 8, "Making a Tentative Career Decision." After emphasizing that career decisions are usually still tentative at this point in the process, the chapter introduces students to a useful, systematic method of analyzing career options. The career analysis exercise in this chapter enables students to select the one career choice that seems most appropriate at this point. Then, in Chapter 9, "Creating a Career Activities Timeline," students both learn about the importance of setting short- and long-term goals related to their career choice and develop specific strategies for accomplishing those goals.

Chapter 10, "Looking and Planning Ahead," presents students with an overview of the stages of career development that follow career exploration and encourages students to refine the career decision-making process as necessary to meet their own individual needs. Finally, for instructors who wish to include a unit on job search strategies, Appendix D provides students with a comprehensive look at the numerous sources available for seeking part-time, volunteer, and full-time employment. Also included in the Appendix are helpful hints about job application procedures and valuable tips for employment interview preparation.

Instructors using this text in class will want to make sure they receive a copy of the *Instructor's Manual and Resource Guide* that accompanies *Making Career Decisions That Count: A Practical Guide*. Both seasoned veterans who have taught career planning and exploration courses for many years and rookies who are teaching the course for the very first time will appreciate the comprehensive nature of the *Instructor's Manual and Resource Guide*. Included in each chapter of the *Instructor's Manual and Resource Guide* (corresponding with each individual chapter of the book) are chapter overviews, learning objectives, key concepts, proposed lecture outlines, suggested activities, discussion questions, and resource materials. The manual also provides instructors with sample course syllabi, transparency masters, a final exam, contact information for publishers of career resource materials, and an updated listing of useful internet sources and World Wide Web sites related to career planning and exploration.

Helping college students make career decisions that will provide them with years of satisfaction and success was first and foremost in my mind as I wrote this book. To that end, it is my sincere hope that the students who read the book and invest an appropriate amount of time and energy into the process will be on the road to making career decisions that count!

ACKNOWLEDGMENTS

I am indebted to numerous individuals whose assistance during the preparation of this book was invaluable. First and foremost, I am extremely grateful to each and every member of the staff at Gorsuch Scarisbrick, Publishers. Their dedication to the success of this project was apparent at every stage of the process. The guidance and support provided by Shari Jo Hehr, Katie Bradford, and Mary Cullen of GSP was especially noteworthy. I also appreciated the helpful comments and suggestions of the three reviewers of the initial manuscript: Garry Klein (Texas A&M University-Corpus Christi), Linda Schlotthauer (Mt. San Jacinto Community College, California), and Dr. Linda Schaf (Miami Dade Community College). I am also grateful for the guidance, direction, and inspiration provided over the years by two of my colleagues, Drs. Charles Healy and Mark Savickas, for whom I hold the highest respect and professional admiration. Most of all, I wish to express my thanks and appreciation to my wonderful wife and eternal soulmate, Denise, and to my five beautiful children: Nicholas, Logan, Kira, Emalise, and Tannan. Without their endless support and encouragement, my dreams would never become reality.

Understanding the World of Work

As you begin the process of making career decisions, it will be important for you to gain a clear understanding of the world of work. The purpose of this chapter is to introduce you to that world. We'll begin the process by discussing a system of categorizing different work environments and careers. Then we will discuss the importance of recognizing certain trends in the world of work and the importance of gathering and organizing occupational information. You'll also have the opportunity in this chapter to reflect on some of your long-term goals as you begin to think about the things you'd like to accomplish over the next several years.

OVERVIEW OF THE WORLD OF WORK

It wasn't long ago that most people in America selected an occupation in their late teens or early twenties and remained in that career for the next 40 to 50 years of their lives. It was a common practice for high school and college graduates to obtain employment with a company soon after graduation and maintain employment with that company until retirement. Decisions about where to work were based primarily on geographical location and family tradition rather than personal values and professional growth.

Today, there's plenty of evidence that times are changing. Most people now struggle during their late teens and early twenties, as well as during other periods in their lives, as they search for the career that promises the most fulfillment and satisfaction. If you're anything like the typical American worker, you'll change jobs somewhere between five and seven times during your working years. Career changes that involve working for a new company, relocating, and rearranging your monthly budget are becoming a reality for more and more people each year. Many of today's high school and college graduates, as well as others who are considering making career changes, are on a quest to find a career that will provide personal satisfaction and the potential for professional growth and development.

The typical American changes jobs five to seven times.

The world of work that you're a part of (or will soon be entering) contains thousands of different occupations. Some occupations require little or no formal training beyond a high school diploma. Others require over a decade of educational training and years of experience. Some occupations involve working with your hands or working outdoors. Others involve working with people or solving complex, scientific problems. Some jobs provide structure and routine in the workplace.

Others provide the opportunity for artistic and creative expression. Determining which occupation is going to provide you with the greatest degree of satisfaction and enjoyment isn't always an easy task.

As you engage in the process of making career decisions, one of the first things you'll need to do is increase your understanding of the world of work. Suppose for a moment that you entered a contest and won a free vacation to the Bahamas. After getting over the initial shock of winning, you'd probably want to know several things about the Bahamas as you prepared for your trip. The average temperature and climate, types of leisure activities, and modes of transportation would all be important to know in order to have a fun and enjoyable vacation. Making career decisions, although perhaps not quite as glamorous as a trip to the Bahamas, also requires important planning and investigation. Just as you'd want to learn about the environment of the Bahamas to prepare for your vacation properly, you'll want to learn about the world of work as you prepare to make career decisions that count.

CLASSIFYING WORK ENVIRONMENTS

There are many different ways to organize the world of work. One of the most well-known systems for classifying work environments was developed by Dr. John L. Holland, whose system includes six primary work environments: Realistic (jobs that involve working with your hands or in outdoor settings), Investigative (jobs that entail searching for solutions to complex problems), Artistic (environments that encourage creativity and personal expression), Social (work settings that provide you with the opportunity to teach and help other people), Enterprising (jobs in which you manage or persuade others), and Conventional (work environments characterized by organization and planning). Dr. Holland's classification system, which is often referred to as the RIASEC model of careers, is used by many career counselors to organize the world of work. You may come across this method of categorizing careers as you are exposed to different assessments and other sources of occupational information over the next several months.

Another well-known system for classifying work environments was developed by Dr. Anne Roe in the 1950s when she discovered that existing classification systems were inadequate. She was troubled that none of the classifications of occupations available at that time seemed to follow any logical principle of classification. Based on years of research and experience, Dr. Roe developed a classification system that includes the following eight occupational groups and work environments.

Service. This work environment is primarily concerned with serving and attending to the personal tastes, needs, and welfare of others. The focus is on doing something to help other people. The types of occupations that fall into this work environment include social work, counseling, and many domestic and protective services.

Business Contact. The occupations included in this work environment are concerned with the face-to-face sale of material goods or services. As in the Service category, person-to-person relationships are important, but in the Business Contact area these relationships are focused on persuading other people to engage in a particular course of action—such as buying a product—rather than on helping others. The types of careers in this work category include sales, public relations, and real estate.

Organization. This work environment is concerned primarily with the organization and efficient functioning of commercial enterprises and government activities, where the quality of person-to-person relationships is formalized. Managerial and white collar jobs in business, industry, and government are included in the Organization work environment.

Technology. The Technology work environment is concerned with the production, maintenance, and transportation of commodities and utilities. Interpersonal relationships are of relatively little value—the focus is on dealing with things as opposed to dealing with people. Occupations in engineering, crafts, machine trades, and transportation belong in the Technology group.

Outdoors. This occupational group includes careers primarily concerned with the cultivation, preservation, and gathering of natural resources and animal welfare. As in the Technology work environment, many Outdoor careers provide few opportunities for emphasizing interpersonal relationships. A wide variety of occupations are appropriately categorized in this work environment, such as applied scientists, landscape architects, forest rangers, and gardeners.

Science. These are the occupations primarily concerned with scientific theory and its application under specified circumstances. Medical doctors, physicists, research psychologists, university professors, and chiropractors are among the many professionals who are directly associated with the Science work environment.

General Culture. Dr. Roe developed the General Culture category to include careers that are primarily concerned with the preservation and transmission of the general cultural heritage. The emphasis in this type of a work environment is on human activities collectively rather than on individual person-to-person relationships. This group includes occupations in education, journalism, law, and careers usually referred to as the humanities (e.g., writing).

Arts and Entertainment. Occupations included in the Arts and Entertainment work environment are those that are primarily concerned with the use of special skills in the creative arts and in the world of entertainment. In this category, the focus is on a relationship between one person (or an organized group) and the general public. A wide range of careers falls into the Arts and Entertainment category, from designers and interior decorators to race car drivers and professional athletes.

To help you get a better sense of Dr. Roe's classification system, Table 1.1 summarizes the eight different work environments she devised.

As we progress through the stages of the career decision-making process, you'll learn more about determining which particular work environments are likely to provide you with the most personal satisfaction and success. But first we have a few other important issues to discuss.

table 1.1 Summary of work environments.

WORK ENVIRONMENT	SAMPLE OCCUPATIONS	CHARACTERISTICS OF PEOPLE WHO LIKE WORKING IN THESE ENVIRONMENTS
Service	Social worker Marriage counselor Police officer Occupational therapist	Enjoy serving and attending to the personal tastes, needs, and welfare of other people; obtain a strong sense of satisfaction from helping and/or protecting other people.
Business Contact	Real estate agent Salesperson Insurance agent Public relations specialist	Enjoy persuading other people to engage in a particular course of action, such as the purchase of a commodity or service.
Organization	Employment manager Accountant Business executive Small-business owner	Enjoy engaging in tasks that involve a high level of organization and precision; often satisfied by supervising or managing others.
Technology	Electrical engineer Mechanic Truck driver Carpenter	Enjoy producing, transporting, and/or fixing things; more satisfied working with tools and objects than with people.
Outdoors	Gardener Wildlife specialist Farmer Horticulturalist	Enjoy working in outdoor settings; often favor working with animals and plants rather than with people.
Science	Chiropractor X-ray technician Dentist Paleontologist	Enjoy working with scientific theory and its application to real-world problems.
General Culture	Lawyer High school teacher Librarian Historian	Enjoy interacting with groups of people in an effort to preserve and/or transmit knowledge and cultural heritage.
Arts and Entertainment	Interior decorator Professional athlete Choreographer Art teacher	Enjoy environments that provide opportunities for artistic expression and/or the use of special skills in an entertainment industry.

TRENDS IN THE WORLD OF WORK

In addition to learning about ways to classify work environments, making effective career decisions also requires you to increase your awareness of trends and forecasts about the future of the world of work. Over the past 15 years, many people have engaged in the process of predicting the economic and demographic employment trends of the future. Some of their predictions have been about as accurate as the words you find in a fortune cookie. Others, however, have provided important information that may be helpful to you.

Get in the habit of going to the library every now and then to read about the world of work and gain a better idea of career projections. Just as you might window shop to check out the latest fashions, skimming through occupational information and projections will give you a clearer picture of the world of work.

It will be important for you to gather various types of information about the world of work during all stages of the career decision-making process. Fortunately,

Skim through occupational information for projections that will give you a clearer picture of the world of work.

there are numerous sources available to you for increasing your understanding of trends in the world of work. Books about job trends and economic expectations can be especially helpful. For example, John Naisbitt and Patricia Aburdene, in their book, *Megatrends 2000*, make a series of observations and predictions regarding the world of work. They point out that the skill requirements of jobs are increasing at a faster rate than the skill levels of employees and managers of those jobs. They also emphasize the rapid growth of small businesses and entrepreneurial endeavors, stating that there will be as many as 40 million individuals working out of their homes, and that up to 85 percent of all employees will be working in companies of 200 employees or fewer by the turn of the century.

Perhaps more relevant to your specific career decisions are Naisbitt and Aburdene's projections about the types of industries that will provide the greatest number of jobs in the future. They include in their list growing industries such as the environmental sciences, health care services, and several other service-oriented careers. Similar projections have been made recently by the U. S. Department of Labor. Based on recent trends, the fastest growing occupations in our country over the next several years include positions in the allied health and service fields (e.g., home health aides, physical therapists, human service workers) and information analysis (e.g., computer systems analysts, operations research analysts).

Of course, these are only projections. Obtaining accurate, up-to-date information about employment opportunities will be valuable for you as you continue to make career decisions. In fact, keeping a close watch on employment trends and changes in the world of work may just well be the key to career satisfaction and success.

In addition to books like *Megatrends 2000* and periodic reports published by the U. S. Department of Labor, there are various other publications that provide a good overview of the world of work. One way to find out about current information is to read magazines, such as *Money* or *Fortune*, that are primarily devoted to covering labor issues. These types of magazines often include feature articles devoted to employment issues and job projections. Even weekly news magazines such as *Time*, *Newsweek*, and *U.S. News & World Report* can supply you with important information about the world of work.

As you begin to gather information, you might also be surprised at how helpful some newspapers can be. Larger newspapers, such as the *Wall Street Journal*, *USA Today*, and the *New York Times*, usually cover stories related to the world of work on a daily basis. Your own local newspaper might be informative as well. Reading through the business section of the local newspaper the other day, I came across an excellent article on local labor trends. The story presented up-to-date information about employment opportunities in various industries located in the local community.

Another quick and easy way to find out what types of careers are on the rise is to see what kinds of training are being offered at your local community college or adult education center. They're likely to be offering the types of training and educational opportunities that people are in need of for adequate job preparation and advancement. The kinds of courses and programs that are popular at a local community college or adult education center indicate the kinds of skills that employers in your area may be looking for.

Yet another source that will become increasingly valuable to you as you narrow your list of career options is the *Occupational Outlook Handbook*, published by the U. S. Department of Labor. The handbook is printed every couple of years and is available at nearly every public and college library. It provides a variety of detailed information about hundreds of occupations. You'll find especially helpful details about working conditions, salary ranges, educational and training requirements, and employment projections for the next several years. The box on the following page is an example of the kind of information you'll find in the *Occupational Outlook Handbook*.

Gather information about the world of work during all stages of the career decision-making process.

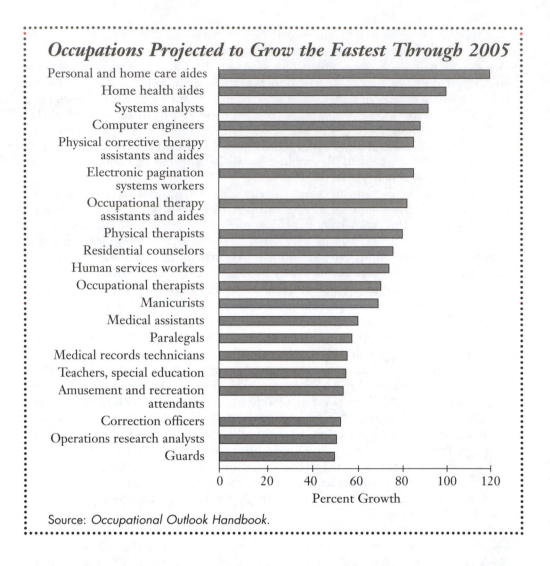

Occupations Projected to Grow the Fastest Through 2005

Source: *Occupational Outlook Handbook.*

The *Dictionary of Occupational Titles*, another sourcebook published by the U. S. Department of Labor that you'll find to be useful, is also available at most libraries. This dictionary includes descriptions of thousands of different occupations and offers helpful information regarding each. You'll learn about using the *Occupational Outlook Handbook* and the *Dictionary of Occupational Titles* as well as many other resources for career exploration in Chapter 6.

GATHERING EMPLOYMENT INFORMATION AND SUPPORT

The kinds of questions you'll want to answer as you gather employment information include the following:

- How many jobs will be available in the career areas that you're considering?
- Will there be ample employment opportunities in the geographical region where you want to live?
- What about salary expectations? Will you make enough money to support your lifestyle needs and wants?
- Is there projected growth within a specific career area or is a decline more realistic?

Along with reading relevant books and magazines, you'll benefit from keeping up to date with current local and global affairs and talking with friends and colleagues about career-related questions.

You should also contact associations and organizations in your area that might be able to offer you support on the basis of your particular background and interests. Many college and university campuses, for example, have organized groups that might be particularly relevant to your life situation. Perhaps joining a student club made up of individuals who share your ethnic background or religious preference would be helpful. Women's centers, international student centers, and offices for students with disabilities are other resources that you may want to consider consulting for support and direction regarding your career choice.

Depending on your level of familiarity and comfort with computers, you might also consider using the Internet as a rich source of occupational information. There are many World Wide Web and "Gopher" sites that can provide you with endless information about employment projections and trends, facts about various careers, and current job openings in various fields. If you have the opportunity to "surf the Net," you'll be sure to find lots of helpful occupational information that'll serve you well throughout the career exploration process.

Some of the information you'll be gathering from these and other sources, such as information about job projections and expected salaries, will become increasingly important to you as you continue the career decision-making process. You might want to consider organizing the information so that it'll be helpful to you in the future. Find a container such as a filing cabinet or a sturdy box that you can use to collect newspaper and magazine articles and keep it where you normally keep your other class materials. Use filing folders or notebooks to separate information into categories. General work trends can be stored in one folder or notebook, employment opportunities can be stored in another notebook, salary expectations can be filed in another, and so forth.

Throughout this book, you'll be encouraged to be as organized as possible as you engage in career decision making. Researchers have consistently found that the most effective career decisions are carried out by those who invest an appropriate amount of time and energy in them. Career decisions can be extremely rewarding and personally fulfilling if you're willing to be an active participant in the process.

If you are an active participant in the process, making career decisions can be rewarding and personally fulfilling.

Consider the cases of Terry and Kelsey, two college graduates who recently prepared to enter the world of work. Both majored in business at a reputable institution in the Midwest. A few months before graduation, Terry and Kelsey both decided that they wanted to find a job on the West Coast. After identifying this goal, Terry began actively engaging in the career decision-making process. In order to learn more about the different types of business-related jobs that were available in various regions of the country, Terry met with several professors at the college and with a few prominent business leaders in the community. They provided Terry with information about the kinds of jobs currently available in the business world and offered helpful advice about job interviewing and resume writing. Terry also began contacting several potential employers on the West Coast, forwarding copies of an updated resume and making follow-up phone calls to inquire about possible openings.

Kelsey, on the other hand, never actively engaged in learning about employment prospects or workforce trends. Kelsey figured that the college placement office would provide that information. There were no meetings with college faculty members, no contacts made with local businesspersons, and no interaction with personnel offices of West Coast companies.

Needless to say, Terry was much more successful in securing a position than Kelsey. Two weeks after graduation, Terry moved to San Francisco and began working for a Fortune 500 firm. Kelsey, however, was unable to obtain employment on the West Coast and is still looking for a job somewhere closer to home. Odds are that Kelsey will probably get a job eventually, but it probably won't provide the degree of job satisfaction and personal fulfillment that might have been realized with proper career planning and preparation.

THE IMPORTANCE OF CAREER PLANNING

Many students often find it hard to understand why it's important, as students, to engage in career decision-making tasks. This seems to be especially true for some freshmen: First-year students often find themselves focusing on the adjustment to college life, dealing with such issues as increased independence and freedom, new responsibilities, academic challenges, and sometimes financial hardships.

There's no question that adjusting to college involves many immediate concerns that need to be dealt with as they arise. Nevertheless, the importance of career planning cannot be emphasized enough. In Chapter 2, you'll learn more about the process of career development and the reasons that career planning is so critical. In the meantime, I want to assure you that the effort you're willing to devote to making career decisions at this point in your life will benefit you for many years to come.

Think for a moment about the role that work and careers play in our lives. On any given day, most people work at least eight or nine hours. Most people also sleep about seven or eight hours a day, which leaves about eight hours for other activities. When you factor in driving time to and from work and time to prepare mentally for work at the start of the day and to wind down once you arrive back home, you quickly begin to realize that a fairly large chunk of your waking hours are spent at work. In fact, it has been suggested that most of us spend the majority of our waking hours during our adult lives engaged in work-related activities. Selecting a career to pursue, then, is certainly not to be taken lightly: It will affect all aspects of your life. That's why it's so important for you to realize that the time and energy you devote to this process now will result in direct dividends to you in the not-so-distant future.

The time and energy you devote to the process of career planning now will result in direct dividends in your not-so-distant future.

To properly set the stage, take a few minutes to complete Exercise 1.1, Long-Range Goal Setting.

As with all of the exercises in this book, it's important that you be honest with yourself. Don't let the expectations of others interfere with your own, personal understanding of who you are and what it is that *you* want. As we'll be discussing later in the book, family influences and the expectations of others can sometimes serve as barriers to effective career decision making. You'll get the most out of these exercises if you're able to reflect on your own personal reactions to the questions that you'll be asked and commit to answering the questions as honestly as you can.

You'll want to complete these exercises at a time when you're free of stress and conflict. Try to find a quiet, peaceful spot for self-reflection. You might try playing soothing music while you complete the exercises or choosing a special physical space that you find particularly comfortable. Sometimes visually imagining a peaceful atmosphere is helpful in this regard. The key is to create an environment that is free of distractions and interruptions. That way you'll be able to think about important issues as you prepare to make the best career decisions that you possibly can.

LONG-RANGE GOAL SETTING

Consider the next 10 to 20 years of your life. There are probably many things that you'd like to accomplish during that period of time. Goals are those things that you're willing to shoot for, even if they seem difficult to obtain. Some of your goals may be best characterized as short-term goals and involve things you'd like to do this month or later this year. Others are probably long-term and include things you'd like to accomplish over the next several years. Many of your goals will be related to your hobbies and interests; others might involve your family and friends. Some are career-related, and others are probably best characterized as leisure activities.

Don't focus too much at this point on career goals. Instead, think of the many different kinds of things that you would like to do in all areas of your life. Be sure to consider personal goals that involve only you and your personal growth and development as well as those goals that involve and influence other people in your life.

A. Take some time to reflect on your future. List below all of the goals (both short-term and long-term) that you'd like to accomplish within the next 20 years or so. Try to state your goals in the language that you usually use. Try not to list your goals in general terms (such as, "I want to be successful."); instead, state your goals in specific ways (such as, "I want to complete my bachelor's degree within the next five years."). Go ahead and dream, too. Even if some of your goals may be idealistic, this is a time to brainstorm about anything and everything that you'd like to accomplish. (We'll worry about realistic expectations later.)

_____

_____

_____

_____

_____

_____

_____

_____

_____

_____

_____

_____

_____

_____

_____

_____

_____

B. Now go back through your list of long-term goals. Place each goal that you've listed into one of the specific time frames listed below.

Goals You Hope to Accomplish Within the Next Year

_____

_____

_____

_____

_____

_____

Goals You Hope to Accomplish Within the Next 2 to 3 Years

_____

_____

_____

_____

_____

_____

_____

Goals You Hope to Accomplish Within the Next 3 to 5 Years

_____

_____

_____

_____

_____

_____

Goals You Hope to Accomplish Within the Next 5 to 10 Years

_____

_____

_____

_____

_____

_____

Goals You Hope to Accomplish Within the Next 10 to 20 Years

_____

_____

_____

_____

_____

_____

_____

C. Over the next several days, try to think of other goals that you might like to accomplish. Add these goals to your list to make it as complete as possible. Allow yourself the flexibility of changing some of your goals, too. These are meant to be guidelines and will serve as the basis for further self-exploration and growth that you'll participate in throughout the career decision-making process.

D. You'll be referring back to your list of long-term goals later in the book. In the meantime, try to remember that your career is just one of the many aspects of your life that deserves attention. Don't forget to devote ample time and energy working toward other personal goals as you continue the quest to make career decisions that count.

2

The Developmental Process of Making Career Decisions

Anyone would agree that before traveling to a particular destination it's a good idea to know how to get there. This is especially true regarding the process of career decision making. If you share the hope that most people do regarding their career, then you're probably looking forward to finding a career that'll bring you satisfaction, stability, and success. In order to reach that destination, it'll be important for you to learn a little bit about how to get there.

The purpose of this chapter is to introduce you to the process of making career decisions that count. In particular, you'll learn about the process of career and life development as conceptualized by the late Dr. Donald Super. You'll learn about the various stages of career development that we experience throughout our lives and the tasks associated with each stage. You'll also have the chance to reflect on past work experiences that you've had and consider their role in your career development. Finally, you'll be given the opportunity to determine which stage of career development you're currently experiencing and which career exploration activities are most relevant to your life situation.

THE PROCESS OF CAREER DEVELOPMENT

When I was in fourth grade, I completed a two-day workshop in my social studies class that was designed to introduce elementary school students to various career options. I remember thinking to myself that the career choice I selected as part of that workshop was going to be the career I would most certainly achieve later in life. Now, over 20 years later, I'm a university professor, a licensed professional counselor, and a father of five children—a far cry from the career choice I selected back in fourth grade (which, by the way, was a Catholic priest!).

Making career decisions is not a static process. Decisions that you make throughout your life, experiences that you have with other people, and the types of environments in which you live all contribute to your career development. Career decision making is a lifelong process that all of us engage in.

If you had met with a career counselor in the early 1900s, that counselor probably would have given you a few tests, analyzed the results, and told you which occupations were worth your time to consider. Odds are that you would have followed the counselor's advice and entered a career that you would have stayed in for the rest of your life. Over the past 50 years or so, career counselors have learned that it's not

Career decision making is a life-long process.

13

that simple. You don't just make one career decision around age 18 and stick with it for life. With rapidly shifting changes in the economy and routine job layoffs in even some of the largest companies across the globe, millions of people find themselves engaging in the career decision-making process all over again every year. That's why many career counselors use the term "career development" when referring to the process of making career decisions. It is a lifelong, developmental process with different activities and tasks along the way. That's why it's so important that you learn about the process involved in making effective career decisions and invest an appropriate amount of time and energy into the process at this point in your life.

SUPER'S THEORY OF CAREER DEVELOPMENT

As with just about any other area of human behavior, counselors and psychologists have developed several different theories in an attempt to explain what goes on during the career development process. One of the most universally accepted theories of career development was generated by Dr. Donald Super, whose theory of career and life development was one of the first to describe career decision making as a developmental process. He believed that career development was primarily a matter of developing and implementing a self-concept.

According to Dr. Super, your self-concept is directly influenced by your personality, abilities, interests, and values. Suppose, for example, that you have the natural ability to listen attentively while others are speaking. Suppose that you're also good at expressing concern for others and helping them find solutions to their problems. These particular attributes might suggest that a career in one of the helping professions would be appropriate for you to consider. If you have little or no interest in such occupations, however, then exploring career options in the helping professions would probably be a waste of your time. Dr. Super argued that the best career choices you can make are those that provide avenues for implementing as many parts of your self-concept as possible.

Your self-concept is a product of the interaction of your personality, interests, skills, and values, and the ways in which you integrate these aspects into your various roles in life.

Your self-concept, according to Dr. Super, is a product of the interaction of your personality, interests, skills, and values, and the ways in which you integrate these aspects of your "self" into your various roles in life. The degree to which your various life roles meet with the approval of others directly influences your self-concept, which changes over time. As you experience new situations, meet new people, and discover new career options, you'll undoubtedly develop a new set of interests, unlock new possibilities of expressing your self-concept, and find new ways of integrating your values into the career choice process.

If you're like most people, it's very likely that somewhere down the road, whether 20 years from now or as early as next year, you'll find yourself in a situation that requires you to reconsider your career direction. It may be the result of economic changes or trends or of new technological advances, or it may simply be "time for a change." Self-concepts change. Your interests and goals may change, too. That's why it's so important for you to learn how to make good career decisions. That way, no matter when the need for another career decision arises, you'll be ready for the challenge.

Dr. Super described career development as consisting of five different stages, which are depicted in Figure 2.1 and summarized in the box on p. 19. Whether you're making career decisions for the first time or recycling through the process for the tenth time, you'll probably find that your current situation fits rather nicely into one or two of these stages.

Growth

The first stage of career development is the **growth** stage. During this stage you form attitudes and behaviors that are important for the development of your self-concept and learn about the general nature of the world of work. According to Dr. Super, our interactions with the social environment influence our personal expectations and goals. Experiences with other people have a direct impact on the development of attitudes and behaviors. Although all children and adolescents are likely to be in the growth stage of career development, they aren't the only ones forming attitudes about careers and learning about the world of work. Many adults find themselves in the growth stage, too.

Lauren, a student I recently worked with, was a 21-year-old woman and was characteristic of someone in the growth stage. She was in her junior year at a university where she had been majoring in education. Lauren was the first person in her family ever to go to college. Her mother and father were extremely supportive of her desire to obtain a college degree, but—primarily because of their lack of college experience—they weren't able to offer Lauren sound advice and direction regarding the educational process.

Nevertheless, Lauren was aware that career counseling and academic advising services were available at the university, so she decided to meet with me to begin that process. One of the first things we talked about was Lauren's decision to major in education. She explained to me that she had simply decided that education would be a good avenue to pursue because there seemed to be a lot of available teaching jobs in the area. It became very clear rather quickly, however, that Lauren was not interested in a career in education. She wanted to find a major that would be more appropriate for her.

As we continued working together, it became apparent that Lauren was still in the process of forming some general attitudes about work and was learning about her self-concept. Although she had not yet begun the actual career exploration process, she was ready and willing to engage in various exploratory activities. Her willingness to take the time and expend the necessary effort to make an effective career decision proved helpful. Today Lauren is successfully employed as a speech pathologist and finds great satisfaction in her work.

Exploration

The second stage of the career development process is **exploration,** considered by many to be the heart of the career decision-making process. Although this book addresses all phases of career development, the focus is on the career exploration component. Dr. Super described the exploration stage as consisting of three major developmental tasks: crystallizing, specifying, and implementing. During the crystallizing task, career "dreaming" occurs. Unrealistic choices are often made at this stage about the kinds of careers that might be pursued. It's not that some of the options identified during the crystallizing period aren't ever actually realized, but most of the selections made at this point are more idealistic than realistic.

A student I worked with several years ago was unquestionably addressing the crystallizing task of exploration when we first met. Jesse had just graduated from high school where he had been active in several different clubs and activities. He had served as the president of his school's Black Students Association, had been successful in speech and debate, and had lettered in several different sports. His mother had convinced him that before going to college he should meet with a career counselor.

As Jesse and I discussed some of the careers that he was interested in, Jesse shared with me his strong desire to achieve several career goals before turning 35. He was confident that he would encounter few problems (if any) in trying to become a U. S. Senator, the CEO of a Fortune 500 company, and an all-pro running back . . . all by the time he turned 35! Somehow he had developed the idea that he could accomplish these goals in less than about 15 years. Although it might have been theoretically possible for Jesse to realize all of his aspirations, it was clear to me that he was still in the process of crystallizing his career identity.

Effective career decision making requires an element of dreaming about a variety of possible career futures. One of your career dreams, for example, might be a very unrealistic option. But there usually comes a time when shifting from several unrealistic career goals to a few focused, more realistic options is a good idea.

The second major developmental task of the exploration stage of career development is specifying. The specifying task involves narrowing down career aspirations to a few occupational areas, with the goal of eventually selecting one of those options for more detailed exploration.

consider Gabriella

Consider the case of Gabriella, a 38-year old woman whose youngest child recently entered kindergarten. After several years of enjoying a career as a homemaker and dabbling in various types of arts and crafts, Gabriella decided to return to college and pursue a new career.

In order to help focus her time and make the best use of her money (this time *she* was paying for school!), Gabriella decided to spend a few months researching information about the various careers that interested her. She gathered information about the world of work and about the specific career areas she thought would be interesting.

Gabriella began the exploration process by considering careers in nursing, teaching, engineering, and court reporting as well as starting up a business of her own. It became apparent to Gabriella during this process that many of the careers she originally considered weren't realistic options for a variety of reasons. Some (e.g., teaching and engineering) required more education than she was willing to complete, and others (e.g., court reporting and nursing) didn't allow her the flexibility that she was seeking in a new career. Gabriella was a prime example of someone working through the specifying task of career exploration.

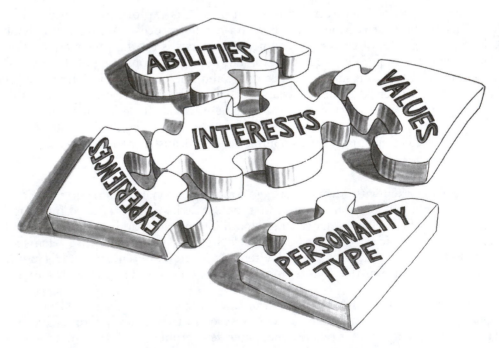

The third and final task of career exploration involves implementing a career choice. The decisions that we make should be based on an increased understanding of our self-concept and the role it plays in effective career decision making. Taking into account our personality, interests, abilities, and values, along with an increased awareness of the world of work and specific employment opportunities, we're better equipped to make quality career decisions and narrow down our career options in a realistic way. Implementing a career choice means beginning training or work related to an occupation. It is an advanced phase of career exploration but not the end of it.

For an example of someone who is experiencing the early stages of implementing, let's return to the case of Gabriella. After narrowing down her list of potential career options during the specifying period of exploration, it was important during the implementing phase for her to focus on those occupations that would fully implement her self-concept. In other words, Gabriella needed to figure out which career options were likely to best fit with her personality, abilities, interests, and values. Careful analysis of information helped Gabriella conclude that starting up her own arts and crafts business was the best option to pursue. Gabriella went on to attend small-business seminars to help her acquire skills associated with running a business.

Some of the ways to accomplish the ever-so-important task of career exploration are described in the chapters that follow. You'll learn how to integrate your self-concept, your knowledge about the world of work, and your understanding of employment opportunities in order to make the best career decisions you possibly can.

Establishment

Once you've completed the exploration stage of career development, you'll enter the **establishment** stage. This stage entails gaining work experiences in occupations associated with your career choice. Work experiences are evaluated as you try to determine the effectiveness of your career decisions. It's a time for "trying out" an occupation once you've made some realistic decisions about your career.

A student I recently worked with, Roberto, was in the process of changing careers. After 15 years of working for the same company, Roberto decided that a career as a draftsperson was no longer as challenging or rewarding as it once had been. After several months of career exploration, during which time Roberto invested a substantial degree of time and energy, he decided to pursue a career in radio broadcasting.

Roberto always had an interest in broadcasting and even worked for a radio station on a part-time basis during college. He had always thought, however, that he might be discriminated against when it came to landing a full-time job in radio because of his Hispanic background. He commented to me that the job market in radio was extremely tough to break into and that few Hispanic people ever made it big in broadcasting.

After Roberto began to realize that there were laws that prohibited discrimination on the basis of one's ethnic and cultural background, he gained the confidence he needed to pursue his interests. Roberto obtained a newscaster position at a local radio station after working for a couple of months as an intern while he finished some course work at the local university. During the first several months of his new job, Roberto was able to get a first-hand sense of what a career in radio broadcasting was all about. He learned about upward mobility possibilities within the company, found out what skills he needed to develop, and gained a clearer perspective about broadcasting careers in general.

During this initial employment phase, Roberto learned that he enjoyed broadcasting even more than he thought he would. He made the decision to continue his pursuit of a career in the broadcasting industry. Today, less than three years later, Roberto is the program director of a local radio station.

Maintenance

The fourth stage of the career development process is the **maintenance** stage, which involves a continual adjustment process as stability within a particular career field becomes a primary objective. During this stage, you continue to improve working conditions and experience growth and development within your chosen career. Of course, it's always possible to realize that you may be in need of a different career direction even once you've entered the maintenance stage of career development.

Consider the case of Darla, a 33-year-old woman who came to my office one afternoon to discuss some of the problems she was facing in her current job. Darla was a regional sales manager for a large paper company. Like many of her friends, Darla had majored in business during college. She recalled her reasons for making the decision to major in business at that time. First, most labor projections that came out during Darla's college years indicated a large increase in business-related occupations. She enjoyed working with other people and thought that business management would be a suitable career choice. Second, Darla had epilepsy and thought that a career in business would provide her with the type of work setting that wouldn't jeopardize her safety or the safety of others.

After eight years with the same company, Darla began to realize that continuing a career in business was not going to provide her with lasting satisfaction. In fact, she was worried that her performance on the job was slipping a bit because of her decreased interest in her career. She couldn't pinpoint exactly why the job was no longer as appealing as it once had been, although she did identify the increase in paperwork and the decrease in interpersonal interactions as particularly disturbing. Furthermore, medications that had recently become available helped Darla gain increased control over her epilepsy, opening up a host of new career possibilities.

When Darla and I first met, she lacked some of the confidence she needed to begin the process of exploring a career change. After engaging in several months of self-reflection and researching information about the world of work, however, Darla was prepared to re-enter the exploration stage of career development and begin making some decisions about possible career options.

Disengagement

Finally, in the last stage of career development, **disengagement,** there is reduced work output. Individuals in the disengagement stage make the decision either to retire or to commit themselves to changing careers altogether. Keeping in mind that career decision making is a lifelong process, it is important to note that disengagement can occur several different times throughout one's work history. The disengagement stage will eventually be a time when you consider retirement from work altogether, but for many people at many different times in their lives disengagement represents a transition from one career to another. Darla eventually reached this stage as she completed career exploration activities and selected a new career as a high school teacher.

Don't forget that this is a developmental process that varies from person to person. You may find yourself in the growth stage of development while one of your

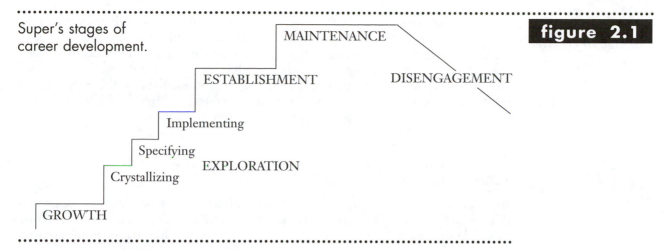

Super's stages of career development.

figure 2.1

Summary of Dr. Super's Stages of Career Development

Stage	Basic Focus Associated with Each Stage
Growth	Learning about the world of work as you increase your awareness of your personality, interests, abilities, and values.
Exploration	Crystallizing, specifying, and implementing a career choice.
Establishment	Gaining work experiences and evaluating your experiences in occupations associated with your career choice.
Maintenance	Developing stability within a chosen career field as you seek ways to improve working conditions and increase skills.
Disengagement	Exploring new ways to spend your time away from your current work environment; might include a career change or retirement from full-time employment.

---

friends of the same age seems to be pretty well established in a career and has moved on to the stage of maintenance. You might be experiencing disengagement from an occupation that you thought you'd be in until retirement. Perhaps with several years to go before retirement, you're now faced with the need to go back and reacquaint yourself with the world of work and begin the process of organized career exploration all over again. If so, don't despair. As mentioned earlier in the chapter, recycling through the stages of career development is becoming more and more of a reality for many people.

DETERMINING WHERE YOU ARE IN THE PROCESS

Recycling through the stages of career development is becoming increasingly common, which emphasizes the importance of learning the skills that are necessary for successful participation in the career decision-making process. You never know when you'll need to recycle through the system. If you learn *how* to engage in effective career exploration, you'll master the tools needed for making good career decisions in the future.

Learning how to engage in effective career exploration will give you the tools you'll need for making good career decisions.

Learning about the process begins as you increase your self-understanding. Exercises 2.1, Your Career Autobiography, and 2.2, Identifying Your Career Needs, are designed to assist you in determining where you are in the career decision-making process. Then, in Chapters 3 and 4, you'll complete several exercises designed to assess your personality, interests, abilities, and values. Each of these exercises is intended to increase your awareness of your self-concept so that you'll be better prepared to embark on the important process of career exploration.

exercise **2.1** YOUR CAREER AUTOBIOGRAPHY

In order to utilize your time and energy most effectively as you engage in the process of making career decisions, you must determine where you are in terms of your own career development. This exercise is designed to assist you in the process of discovering which developmental stages are the focus of your current career and life situation.

In the spaces provided on the next several pages, you're invited to write a brief, informal career autobiography of experiences in your life that are relevant to your career development. You might begin by describing your career dreams, those occupations you might have named when responding to the question, "What do you want to be when you grow up?" Discuss how your career dreams have influenced some of the decisions and job experiences you've had up to now.

Also be sure to list any jobs or other work experiences you've had in the past. Include in your list any volunteer work or internship activities. Explain how these experiences have provided you with some feedback about your interests and skills. Hobbies, leisure activities, and athletic participation should also be included in your autobiography.

You should be sure to mention any significant events in your life that have played a role in previous career decisions. The ways that your cultural and ethnic background, socioeconomic status, gender, and religious beliefs have influenced your career decisions would be especially important to reflect upon as you complete this exercise.

Conclude your story with a discussion of the various career issues you're facing today, such as your current job or educational status, questions that you have about your future, and so forth.

Take some time to think about what you might want to include in your autobiography. You might even wait a couple of days before completing this exercise so that you can review some of the significant events in your life that have affected prior career choices you've made. This is an exercise in which self-reflection is especially important. However, if you're not sure whether to include certain information, then include it. It's better to have a little more information in your story than to leave out a potentially important detail.

Although there are many students I've worked with in the past who have no problem at all discussing their career development, I've also worked with many others—especially first-year college students—who often claim that there isn't much for them to include in a career autobiography. They'll often mention that they've only held a couple of part-time jobs over the years and haven't had any real work experience worth mentioning.

Perhaps you find yourself in the same boat. But part-time work experiences are certainly an important part of your career autobiography.

How much you've enjoyed previous work experiences—whether full- or part-time—plays an important role in thinking about the kinds of careers that are interesting to you. All of your thoughts and feelings about making career decisions should be included in your autobiography.

Topics to Include in Your Autobiography

- Career Dreams
- Previous Paid Employment Experiences
- Volunteer Experiences
- Internship Activities
- Hobbies
- Leisure Interests
- Athletic Participation
- Ethnic Background and Heritage
- Socioeconomic Status
- Gender Roles
- Current Educational Status
- Current Employment Status
- Questions About Your Future
- Careers that Seem Interesting to You
- Career-Related Issues You're Currently Facing

Career Autobiography

_____

_____

_____

_____

_____

_____

_____

_____

_____

_____

_____

_____

_____

_____

_____

_____

_____

_____

_____

_____

_____

_____

_____

_____

_____

_____

_____

_____

_____

_____

_____

_____

_____

_____

_____

_____

_____

_____

_____

_____

_____

_____

_____

_____

_____

If you need more space, continue your autobiography on additional sheets of paper.

exercise 2.2 IDENTIFYING YOUR CAREER NEEDS

(Make sure you've completed your Career Autobiography before proceeding with this exercise.)

By putting together your autobiography, you've probably learned something about yourself and about your career development in particular. You can significantly increase awareness of your self-concept by taking the time to reflect on past experiences and consider the decisions you're currently making.

In order to determine which developmental stage you're currently experiencing, go back to your autobiography and highlight (or draw a circle around) any information that describes your **current situation.** Although most of this material will be at the end of your autobiography, there may be some reference to your current career status in other parts of your autobiography as well. Any information that explains issues you're facing or the decisions you're hoping to make in the near future should be marked in some way to signify their relevance to your current situation.

Now compare the information you've highlighted with the chart below that summarizes the various stages of development that have been presented in this chapter. You should have a pretty good idea of where you are in the career development process once you've completed this exercise. Check the boxes that correspond with the stages of career development that you most directly identify with at this time.

In the far right column of the table, you'll notice the career needs you're likely to be facing at this point in your career development. Also listed are the chapters of this book that you'll find especially helpful in your current developmental stage.

SUMMARY OF CAREER DEVELOPMENT STAGES

STAGE OF CAREER DEVELOPMENT	TYPES OF TASKS	SAMPLE AUTOBIOGRAPHY STATEMENTS	CAREER NEEDS
Growth ☐	(1) Forming work attitudes and behaviors	"I'm trying to figure out what I really want to do in life."	Learn about the world of work in general (Chapters 1 & 6)
	(2) Learning about the world of work	"I'm gathering lots of information about the job market."	Find out about trends in the labor market (Chapters 1 & 6)
			Get an idea of projections for some careers (Chapters 1 & 6)
			Increase self-understanding and awareness (Chapters 2–4)
			Determine your relevant interests and abilities (Chapter 3)
			Familiarize yourself with your work values (Chapter 4)
Exploration ☐	(1) Identifying career dreams	"I've always wanted to be a . . ."	Reflect on the careers you've dreamed about (Chapter 3)
	(2) Trying to narrow a list of career possibilities	"There are several occupations that interest me. I need to figure out which are realistic."	Develop a list of career options (Chapters 3, 4, & 5) Narrow your list to realistic options (Chapter 5)
	(3) Determining your self-concept as it relates to the career decision-making process	"I'm not sure if I'll be really happy if I pursue *that* career."	Match your self-concept with a career choice (Chapter 5)
		"I'm wondering if it will be a career that I will enjoy for years to come."	Gather information about various careers (Chapters 5 & 6)

(continued)

	(4) Deciding which career options to research	"Now I need to figure out which careers I need more information about."	Read about job trends for specific career areas (Chapter 6)
			Gather information about options you're pursuing (Chapter 6)
			Identify potential barriers to career success (Chapter 7)
			Learn ways to overcome barriers to success (Chapter 7)
			Identify support for decisions you're making (Chapter 7)
			Make a tentative career decision (Chapter 8)
			Set some clearly defined career choice goals (Chapter 9)
			Set up a timeline for realizing your goals (Chapter 9)
Establishment ❐	(1) Gaining work experiences related to your career choice	"I'm currently working in a job that will allow me the chance to see if I really want to pursue that career or not."	Continue the process of self-awareness (Chapters 3, 4, & 10)
	(2) Trying to determine the value of your choices	"Now that I'm working in this field, I'm not too sure that my job is really meeting my needs."	Decide if your values are being addressed (Chapter 4)
	(3) Continuing to increase self-understanding	"I'm learning a lot about myself as I continue to work in this field."	Set goals for gaining new experiences in an area (Chapter 9)
	(4) Beginning to stabilize within a career	"I'm satisfied with where I am at this point in my career."	Evaluate current job satisfaction (Appendix E)
Maintenance ❐	(1) Determining whether your current career situation is providing adequate satisfaction and fulfillment	"Lately I've been trying to determine whether I'm truly happy doing what I'm doing."	Determine whether to remain in a current job (Chapters 3–5)
		"I'm starting to think that maybe I should find out about other careers."	Evaluate current job satisfaction (Appendix E)
	(2) Searching for ways to increase job mobility	"Right now I'm trying to determine whether there is any chance that I might be promoted in the future."	Learn about other careers related to your job (Chapters 5 & 6)
	(3) Learning about other career options related to your current occupation	"I'm hoping that I will find some other jobs similar to my current one that I can consider applying for."	Learn about methods for locating new job opportunities (Appendix D)
Disengagement ❐	(1) Considering a new job or career change	"I'm pretty sure that I want to find a new job. This one is getting old."	Determine the appropriateness of a career change (Chapters 3–5; Appendix E)
	(2) Preparing for retirement	"I'm looking forward to golfing six days a week."	

As you can see, the main focus of this book is on the process of career exploration. So, now that you're aware of how the chapters that follow apply to your particular developmental stage, let the games begin!

3

Assessing Your Personality, Interests, Abilities, and Experiences

Imagine graduating from high school or college without ever having taken a test. Although the thought of never having to take a test may be appealing to you, you probably have a pretty good idea why we take tests. In most school settings, tests give us and our teachers a chance to measure our knowledge. Weekly spelling and vocabulary tests in elementary school, for example, assess how well we learned material that was presented to us in class. Of course, tests and assessments aren't always given to people in order to grade them on their ability to recall specific information they've been taught. Many tests are designed to help people learn more about who they are and what makes them different from everyone else.

As you may recall from Chapter 2, Dr. Donald Super developed a theory of career development that emphasizes implementing as many parts of your self-concept as possible when making career decisions. In order for you to seek career choices that will provide you with the maximum opportunity to implement your self-concept, you first need to know what makes you who you are. The purpose of this chapter, then, is to assist you in the process of increasing your awareness of your self-concept: examining your personality, interests, abilities, and experiences. Then you can prepare to make career decisions that will maximize your chances of success and satisfaction. (Depicted in the drawing on p. 16, values are also integral to a person's self-concept. Values are discussed in more detail in Chapter 4.)

THE IMPORTANCE OF CAREER ASSESSMENT

A student I recently worked with, LaTonya, came to me to discuss some of her career concerns. She was attending a local university where she was about to complete her sophomore year, but she was having a difficult time deciding on a major. No matter how hard she tried, she was not able to figure out which one major out of all the options available to her would be the absolute best choice.

LaTonya had narrowed down her list of options to three different career fields, including careers in business, education, and social work. When I asked her how she had arrived at these particular careers, she said that her choices had been based on advice from friends and family members. Her mother was encouraging LaTonya to

consider
La Tonya

25

go into business because of the money-making potential. Her father wanted her to become an elementary school teacher because he was confident that she would have a great time working with children. And LaTonya's friends were trying to convince her that she would be great at social work because of her concern for others and her desire to help people.

I asked LaTonya what she was hoping to accomplish in her eventual career choice, and she had a rather difficult time explaining precisely what it was that *she*—independent from family members and friends—really wanted. I realized LaTonya hadn't engaged in an analysis of her own likes, dislikes, skills, and abilities, nor had she considered how some of her past experiences could help her make a better career decision.

LaTonya and I worked together for several weeks with the primary purpose of increasing her awareness of her self-concept. She completed several exercises, including assessments of personality, interests, skills, and abilities. Then we worked on searching for careers that maximized LaTonya's chances for implementing as many parts of her self-concept as possible. As it turned out, LaTonya was more interested in a career in public relations than in any of the careers her family and friends were encouraging her to consider.

Career counselors have long recognized the importance of assessing personality, interests, skills, and experiences when working with students of all ages. It's not uncommon, for instance, for career counselors to administer several different inventories or assessments to students who seek their assistance. The results of such tests often provide both the students and the counselor with important information to consider in the career decision-making process.

Whenever I think about the importance of assessment in career decision making, I'm usually reminded of Gonzalo, a student I worked with several years ago. Gonzalo was a 37-year-old electrical engineer employed as a shift supervisor at a large engineering firm in the Southwest. After 13 years at the same company, even though he had received promotions over the years, Gonzalo was no longer as satisfied with his career as he had once been.

I asked Gonzalo why this was so, and he explained that while he still enjoyed the emphasis on math and science that a career as an electrical engineer provided, he didn't enjoy working in a supervisory role, and the work wasn't fun any more.

Gonzalo told me about a new interest he had developed: working with adolescents. Gonzalo had volunteered to serve as a Cub Scout leader in his community and had discovered that he thoroughly enjoyed working with youth. As a result, Gonzalo had also volunteered to coach a soccer team, and he looked into the possibility of increasing his involvement in other youth activities in the community. Apparently, Gonzalo had developed an interest in working with adolescents but was unable to find an easy way to integrate that new interest into his existing work environment.

Gonzalo completed several personality, interest, and skills inventories which helped him make the eventual decision to pursue a career teaching high school math and coaching. Gonzalo might never have sought a career in education if he hadn't been willing to invest the time and energy necessary to re-evaluate his self-concept. The career assessment results verified his interests and abilities in working with adolescents.

Our interests aren't the only aspects of ourselves that change: our job-related skills also change over time. That's why periodic assessments of all aspects of our self-concept—our personality, interests, abilities, *and* experiences—can be so important when we're making career decisions.

ASSESSMENT OF PERSONALITY

One of the best ways to begin the process of gathering information about yourself is to consider your own, personal temperament or personality type. Your *temperament* or *personality* is your way of perceiving the world and the things that happen to you. It's the way you generally tend to handle things. As you may already know, psychologists have found that our personalities are directly linked to attitudes and behavior and influence our beliefs and actions.

One way to learn more about your personality is to complete a personality or temperament inventory. One of the most popular measures of personality used to help students make career decisions is the Myers-Briggs Type Inventory, commonly referred to as the MBTI. If you have the chance to complete the MBTI, take advantage of that opportunity. Knowing your psychological type allows you to increase your awareness of your self-concept.

The MBTI is based on a theory of psychological types developed by Dr. Carl Jung. According to Dr. Jung, there are four different personality dimensions that interact with one another to determine a person's psychological type. These four dimensions of personality are briefly described in the accompanying box.

Your particular personality or psychological type is determined by combining your preferences regarding each of these four dimensions. For example, if you're the type of person who focuses your perception and judgments primarily on the external world of actions, objects, and persons (Extraversion), perceives information primarily in terms of meanings, concepts, and relationships (Intuition), makes judgments on the basis of personal, social, and subjective values (Feeling), and prefers flexibility, openness, and a free flow of information when dealing with the external

Your temperament or personality is your way of perceiving the world and the things that happen to you.

Four Dimensions of Personality

Extraversion vs. Introversion

(E) Extraversion: Focusing your perceptions and judgments about things based on the external world of actions, objects, and persons

(I) Introversion: Focusing your perceptions and judgments about things based on the internal world of concepts and ideas

Sensing vs. Intuition

(S) Sensing: Perceiving information primarily in terms of concrete facts and details

(N) Intuition: Perceiving information primarily in terms of meanings, concepts, and relationships

Thinking vs. Feeling

(T) Thinking: Making judgments and decisions primarily on the basis of logic and objective analysis

(F) Feeling: Making judgments and decisions primarily on the basis of personal, social, and subjective values

Judgment vs. Perception

(J) Judgment: Preferring order, closure, and structure when dealing with others

(P) Perception: Preferring flexibility, openness, and a free flow of information when dealing with others

world (Perception), then your psychological type would be characterized as Extraversion-Intuition-Feeling-Perception, or ENFP for short.

The developers of personality assessment instruments have found that certain types of work environments and careers are more attractive to persons of certain personality types. This is valuable information for individuals exploring career choices. This knowledge allows you to begin to think about who you are and how you fit into a work environment.

Exercise 3.1 will allow you to learn more about your personality and show you how this newfound information about yourself can help you make a satisfying career choice.

WHAT'S MY TYPE?

Step I.

For each of the following pairs of statements, check the option that describes you best. You *must* select one of the statements in each pair. There are no right or wrong answers.

Section One

1. _____ I like to be around other people.   _____ I prefer spending time alone.

2. _____ I prefer working on team projects.   _____ I'd rather complete a project on my own.

3. _____ I often ask others for their opinions about decisions I have to make at work.   _____ I usually make important decisions at work on my own.

Section Two

4. _____ I like work that involves precise objectives and clearly defined details.   _____ I prefer work that is less defined and that requires very little precision.

5. _____ I enjoy routine in the work place.   _____ I dislike doing the same tasks at work every day.

6. _____ I don't rely too much on inspiration when I'm involved in a project.   _____ Inspiration plays an important role in my work.

Section Three

7. _____ Most of the decisions I make at work are based on rational thinking and an analysis of the situation.   _____ I tend to make decisions at work based on what feels right to me at the time.

8. _____ I don't usually focus too much on others' feelings about decisions that I make at work.   _____ I am usually very aware of others' feelings about decisions that I make at work.

9. _____ I'm not too concerned about pleasing other people in the workplace.   _____ I enjoy making others feel good about themselves at work.

Section Four

10. _____ I like making definite plans about my future. _____ I prefer leaving my options open regarding future plans.

11. _____ I like making well-defined decisions about things. _____ I don't like making definite decisions about things.

12. _____ I prefer rigid, clear-cut directions when working on a task. _____ I'd rather work on a task that's less clearly defined and allows for flexibility and change.

Step II.   Scoring

As you may have figured out while completing the exercise, each section represents a different personality dimension. Section One statements reflect the Extraversion vs. Introversion dimension of personality. The statements on the left side represent Extraversion, whereas the statements on the right side represent Introversion. Section Two statements represent the Sensing vs. Intuition dimension, with statements on the left side reflecting a Sensing orientation and statements on the right side reflecting an Intuition orientation. Section Three statements represent Thinking (statements on the left side) vs. Feeling (statements on the right side), and Section Four statements reflect Judgment (left) vs. Perception (right).

To get a rough estimate of your personality type (realizing that your true psychological type can only be reliably assessed by a lengthier assessment, such as the MBTI), determine which personality orientation in each section you tend to associate with by figuring out which types of statements you marked as describing you best. If, for example, you checked off two statements on the left side of Section One and only one statement on the right side, or all three statements on the left side, then you probably have Extraversion (E) dominance on that particular dimension.

Indicate below your preferences based on your analysis of preferences in each domain:

Section One

_____ Extraversion (E)   _____ Introversion (I)

Section Two

_____ Sensing (S)   _____ Intuition (N)

Section Three

_____ Thinking (T)   _____ Feeling (F)

Section Four

_____ Judgment (J)   _____ Perception (P)

Now place the letter of your preference in each dimension (in order) in the spaces below:

Your Type: _____ _____ _____ _____
            (Section   1   2   3   4)

Step III.   Careers and Personality Type

You may recall from an earlier discussion that the developers of personality assessment instruments have found certain types of work environments and careers are more attractive to some people than they are to others, depending on personality type. Persons who identify more with Extraversion than Introversion, for example, are probably going to be much more satisfied in a career that involves a lot of opportunity to work with others in a group or team setting. On the other hand, individuals with an Introversion orientation are probably much more satisfied in careers that maximize opportunities to work alone or in one-on-one situations.

Sensing individuals usually like careers that involve concrete facts and data, whereas intuitive types probably find careers with less structure and detail much more rewarding. As you might imagine, individuals with a thinking orientation prefer careers that involve logical reasoning, whereas individuals with a feeling orientation prefer careers that involve feelings and emotions. Finally, it follows that persons who possess a judgment orientation like careers with a high degree of organization, structure, and routine, whereas persons who possess a perceiving orientation prefer careers with a high degree of flexibility and spontaneity.

In his book, *Introduction to Type and Career*, Allen Hammer put together a list of specific careers that persons with certain psychological types often find most attractive. This list can be found in Appendix A at the back of the book. As you look through the list of occupations that directly match your psychological type, don't be surprised if a few of the occupations don't seem to fit your personality perfectly. Even though you share many aspects of your personality with other people who share your psychological type, you're not necessarily going to prefer *all* of the careers that are generally attractive to folks with that type.

List below any of the careers under your psychological type in Appendix A that seem interesting to you. If you've had the opportunity to complete the MBTI, include any occupations generated from the actual MBTI report that you'd like to learn more about.

_____

_____

_____

_____

_____

We'll be taking another look at the importance of your personality and the careers you've listed above a little later on in the exploration process.

ASSESSMENT OF INTERESTS

The most commonly administered career assessments are the group of tests referred to as interest inventories. These types of assessments include popular measures such as the Self-Directed Search and the Strong Interest Inventory. Interest inventories are designed to give students the chance to think about their interests in a variety of leisure activities, academic areas, and work environments. An individual's particular interests are then compared to the interests of other persons who have completed the inventory and who are satisfied with their career choice.

Say, for example, that a first-year college student, Malcolm, completes the Strong Interest Inventory. After Malcolm completes the inventory, it is either sent to the test publisher for scoring and analysis or scored on-site by on-line computer services. Malcolm's responses to the various questions on the inventory are compared to the answers that individuals representing hundreds of different careers provided when they completed the very same inventory. This comparison group is made up of workers who have experienced a high degree of job satisfaction, success, and stability in their career. In other words, Malcolm's responses are compared with the responses of individuals who are satisfied with their careers, successful in their careers, and who have been established within their careers for several years.

Interest inventories give you the chance to think about your interests in leisure activities, academic areas, and work environments.

If Malcolm's inventory profile is similar to the profile of an accountant, for example, then the report generated for Malcolm will suggest that he explore a career in that field. If, on the other hand, his responses differ greatly from the types of responses provided by most accountants, then the report would indicate that a career as an accountant would probably not be very fulfilling for Malcolm.

As you might imagine, results from interest inventories can provide you with helpful information in making some initial career decisions. By learning which career areas are compatible with your interests, you can explore specific opportunities that exist within that particular area. Exercise 3.2, Career Dreaming, and Exercise 3.3, Activities Ratings, will provide you with the type of increased awareness of your interests that will help you narrow down your career options.

CAREER DREAMING   **3.2**

As you may recall from Chapter 2, Dr. Super used the term *crystallizing* to refer to some of the career decisions we often make when we're at the beginning of the exploration process. I can remember being seven or eight years old and telling everyone that I was going to be a dentist when I grew up. I was simply fantasizing or dreaming about a career that I found interesting. Even at a very young age, we have at least some idea of what we like and dislike, even though many of us eventually select careers that are very different from those early career fantasies.

This exercise gives you the chance to fantasize again, to consider those careers that you would pursue if there were no barriers to prevent you from doing so. That's right! It's time to dream again. Forget for a moment about the many reasons a particular career goal would be difficult to realize. Instead, allow yourself to dream about the careers you'd pursue if there were *no reasons at all* to stop you from doing so. List your current career fantasies and dreams in the spaces below:

Career Dreams

1. _____

2. _____

3. _____

4. _____

5. _____

6. _____

7. _____

You'll return to this exercise in Chapter 5 as you begin to integrate results of various assessments designed to help you narrow down your list of career options. In the meantime, if you think of any other career "dreams" in the next few days, feel free to add them to this list.

ACTIVITIES RATINGS

To complete this exercise, simply rate your interest in each of the following activities. Use the scale shown below to rate your interest:

1	2	3	4	5
not interested at all	not very interested	neutral	somewhat interested	very interested

Activity	Rating
1. Visiting a scientific laboratory	_____
2. Taking a business class	_____
3. Keeping track of schedules and details	_____
4. Thinking about philosophy	_____
5. Enforcing safety regulations	_____
6. Hiking in the mountains	_____
7. Analyzing statistical results	_____
8. Training other people to do something	_____
9. Expressing your ideas in an original way	_____
10. Playing outdoors	_____
11. Maintaining financial records	_____
12. Selling products or ideas	_____
13. Editing a newspaper article	_____
14. Typing, filing, and record keeping	_____
15. Repairing a broken machine	_____
16. Working in a garden	_____
17. Analyzing theoretical problems	_____
18. Following established office procedures	_____
19. Teaching adolescents	_____
20. Solving complex problems	_____
21. Working with machines or tools	_____
22. Scheduling activities or events	_____
23. Playing a musical instrument	_____
24. Marketing a product or idea	_____
25. Reading *Popular Science* magazine	_____
26. Assisting others who need help	_____
27. Fixing a broken engine	_____
28. Painting or sketching	_____
29. Teaching children	_____

30. Farming land for crops   _____

31. Playing competitive sports   _____

32. Working in a social service agency   _____

33. Promoting a new product   _____

34. Expressing yourself in creative ways   _____

35. Designing an efficient electrical system   _____

36. Reading *Business Week* magazine   _____

37. Debating a legal issue   _____

38. Driving a tractor   _____

39. Taking a human relations course   _____

40. Driving a large diesel truck   _____

As with the other exercises in this chapter, we'll be scoring and integrating the results of this exercise when we get to Chapter 5.

ASSESSMENTS OF ABILITIES AND EXPERIENCES

In addition to personality and interest assessments, skills and aptitude tests are common in career development. These types of tests are designed to evaluate an individual's abilities in several different work-related domains. Some of these assessments are merely self-ratings of skill and might involve nothing more than rating how good you think you are at certain work-related tasks. Other assessments, such as the Armed Services Vocational Aptitude Battery and the Differential Aptitude Test, involve a detailed analysis of demonstrated work-related skills and abilities.

Career counselors will sometimes suggest that students complete a battery of ability and aptitude tests to gather information about particularly relevant work-related skills. The information provided by the results of such tests usually helps us make important decisions about the practicality of certain career choices and can suggest careers for exploration that we might not have otherwise considered.

Consider the case of Shelley, a sophomore attending a large university in Southern California. Shelley took college very seriously. Her family was unable to help her financially, so Shelley had to work 30 hours a week while going to college. She wanted to be very organized in her career planning and therefore wasted no time beginning the process of career exploration.

Shelley was fairly sure that she wanted to pursue a career in either medicine or law, but she was having a difficult time deciding, and she met with me for assistance with the process. When I asked her how she had developed an interest in medicine and law, Shelley described the series of personality and interest inventories (which included the MBTI, Self Directed Search, and the Strong Interest Inventory) that she had completed during her first year in college. The results of the inventories consistently revealed that careers in medicine and law were directly related to her hobbies and interests. Shelley was especially interested in professions that would provide her the opportunity to help others, and she was confident after interviewing various doctors and lawyers that both professions would be rewarding.

Until our interactions, however, Shelley didn't have a really clear sense of her skills associated with law and medicine. Most of the classes she had completed during her first year were general education courses. Although she enjoyed the classes, they didn't provide her with the chance to explore her abilities in areas directly related to medicine and law. We agreed that completion of an aptitude assessment would be helpful.

In particular, Shelly agreed to take the Differential Aptitude Test, or DAT. The DAT is a multiple aptitude battery designed to measure a person's ability to learn or to succeed in certain areas. Results of the tests indicated that Shelley possessed many of the skills associated with a career in medicine. She scored exceptionally high on the Numerical Reasoning and Abstract Reasoning scales of the DAT, providing evidence of her math and science ability and her ability to solve complex problems.

Although Shelley possessed many of the skills related to a career in law, as revealed by her moderately high scores on the Verbal Reasoning and Language Use scales, she demonstrated somewhat lower skills in many of these areas compared to her performance in the domains related to a career in medicine. Our discussions also revealed that Shelley was less confident in her ability to engage in oral arguments and debate than in her ability to diagnose problems and work on investigative tasks. The information about Shelley's skills and abilities that we gathered from the assessments, along with other discussions we had, helped her make the eventual decision to enroll in the college's pre-med program.

As you engage in the process of making career decisions, it will be helpful for you to assess your strengths and weaknesses and learn to integrate such information into your career choice. As with assessments of personality and interests, if you have access to a reliable and valid of skills and abilities, you should consider completing such an assessment. In the meantime, Exercise 3.4, Linking the Past to the Present, and Exercise 3.5, How Well Do You Do What You Do?, will help you begin to think about the ways that past experiences have helped you acquire certain work-related skills.

3.4 LINKING THE PAST TO THE PRESENT

To complete this exercise, simply evaluate your experience engaging in the various activities listed below. There may be some activities that you've not yet experienced, but you probably have at least some experience with most. For those activities that you haven't had any experience with, estimate how much you *think* you'd enjoy the activity. Use the following scale when rating your experiences:

1	2	3	4	5
do not enjoy at all	do not enjoy very much	neutral	enjoy somewhat	enjoy very much

Activity | Rating

1. Creating art work   _____

2. Serving other people   _____

3. Promoting a new product   _____

4. Hiking and camping   _____

5. Solving scientific problems   _____

6. Working with tools   _____

7. Managing other people's work   _____

8. Teaching a child how to read   _____

9. Playing a musical instrument   _____

10. Doing volunteer work   _____

11. Conducting research   _____

12. Planting flowers in a garden   _____

13. Selling life insurance   _____

14. Drawing or sketching a picture   _____

15. Hunting and fishing   _____

16. Debating legal ideas   _____

17. Solving a crime   _____

18. Reading science books   _____

19. Entertaining other people   _____

20. Discussing the world of business   _____

21. Repairing machines   _____

22. Collecting scientific data   _____

23. Selling a home   _____

24. Organizing information   _____

25. Driving a taxi   _____

26. Rebuilding an engine or appliance   _____

27. Thinking about the meaning of life   _____

28. Selling products   _____

29. Filing office records   _____

30. Working outdoors   _____

31. Writing a news story   _____

32. Working in a medical laboratory   _____

33. Decorating a room   _____

34. Building something from scratch   _____

35. Doing your taxes   _____

36. Helping someone choose a career   _____

37. Selling automobiles   _____

38. Designing a home   _____

39. Harvesting crops   _____

40. Announcing the news on the radio   _____

HOW WELL DO YOU DO WHAT YOU DO?

To complete this exercise, indicate your skill level for each of the activities listed below. Use the following scale for rating your skills:

1	2	3	4	5
no skill at all	very little skill	average skill	high skill	very high skill

Activity	Skill Rating
1. Helping others with their personal problems	_____
2. Working with animals/livestock	_____
3. Understanding a complex legal argument	_____
4. Managing and supervising people	_____
5. Promoting a product or company	_____
6. Creating art work	_____
7. Understanding the meaning of a philosophical concept	_____
8. Operating a farm	_____
9. Typing and filing documents	_____
10. Fixing broken mechanical objects	_____
11. Designing the interior of a home	_____
12. Solving math problems	_____
13. Developing friendships	_____
14. Playing a musical instrument	_____
15. Convincing someone to buy a product	_____
16. Influencing other people	_____
17. Understanding others' feelings	_____
18. Understanding how a machine works	_____
19. Teaching other people	_____
20. Managing data systems	_____
21. Solving scientific problems	_____
22. Reporting the news	_____
23. Showing compassion to others	_____
24. Growing plants and flowers	_____
25. Selling life insurance	_____
26. Working in a construction setting	_____
27. Diagnosing a medical illness	_____
28. Proofreading accurately	_____
29. Focusing on organizational needs	_____

30. Handling emergency situations   _____

31. Landscaping a plot of land   _____

32. Understanding a scientific theory   _____

33. Reassembling an engine   _____

34. Engaging in competitive athletic events   _____

35. Working as a car salesperson   _____

36. Researching a scientific topic of interest   _____

37. Building kitchen cabinets   _____

38. Operating farm equipment   _____

39. Developing a marketing plan to sell a new product   _____

40. Performing in front of a large audience   _____

When we get to Chapter 5, we'll score and interpret the results of this and the other exercises in the chapter. But first you'll need to explore your values and gain a better understanding of how your values influence your career decisions. This is the focus of Chapter 4.

Career counselors specialize in helping people in all aspects of the career-development process.

OTHER TYPES OF CAREER ASSESSMENT

In addition to traditional personality and interest inventories and measures of aptitudes and abilities, test developers have created many other assessments to help us make the most well-informed career decisions that we possibly can. One such measure is a recently developed inventory that combines assessments of interests and skills into one—the Campbell Interest and Skills Survey.

The author of the Campbell Interest and Skills Survey, Dr. David Campbell, has several years of experience in the development of interest inventories. This new measure may prove particularly helpful in providing persons with valuable information about how interests and skills can be combined with one another when making career decisions.

There are a host of other assessments that career counselors can use to help students make well-informed career decisions, too. *Career counselors* are professional counselors who specialize in helping people in all aspects of the career development process. Most career counselors have master's degrees in counseling and have completed several years of professional training. You might find it very helpful at some point during your career development to seek the assistance of a career counselor and participate in a thorough evaluation of your personality, interests, skills, and values.

Remember that assessments of our personality, interests, abilities, and experiences are helpful because they increase our understanding of ourselves. This isn't to say that we don't already have a good idea of who we are, but we don't often think about our personality, interests, and skills as they relate to making career decisions. Without such information our career decisions are likely to be far from satisfying and our ability to fully integrate aspects of our self-concept much less effective.

4

Recognizing the Importance of Your Values

Just as assessments of our personality, interests, and abilities are important in the process of making career decisions, so are assessments of our values. Making a career decision based only on what we like and what we're good at can easily lead to job dissatisfaction and unhappiness. That's probably why Dr. Super believed that knowing about our own personal values and understanding how those values influence our happiness and satisfaction are such important components of making good career decisions.

As you begin to narrow your list of career possibilities, you will benefit from evaluating your values. The primary purpose of this chapter is to introduce you to the roles that values play in effective career decision making. After learning about different types of values and their influence in your life, you'll be provided with the opportunity to begin to consider how your personal values can be integrated into your career decision.

THE ROLE OF WORK-RELATED VALUES

Over the past several years we've heard quite a bit about values, including everything from the importance of family values to the ways that values are depicted in the media. We've seen politicians whose morals and values have been challenged by their peers. We've read news accounts of business executives and government leaders who have lost their positions of status and power because of behavior that society has deemed immoral or unethical.

As we talk about values, it's helpful to recognize the many different ways we can define them. Some of us think of values as morals or ethics. Others consider values to be important beliefs and opinions. I've even heard values defined as those beliefs that are such an important part of who you are that you'd be willing to die for them. Sounds pretty strong, doesn't it? But such a definition helps us realize why ignoring values can lead to career decisions that we're likely to regret over time.

Most career counselors challenge students to think over those aspects of the work environment about which they have especially strong feelings. Students are encouraged to think about the types of work and the qualities of work environments that really matter to them. The increased awareness that you'll get from this type of self-reflection can often make a world of difference when it comes time to make some final decisions about your career.

I worked with a student several years ago for whom this was especially true. Hai had made the decision to return to school after several years of working in a job that produced very little satisfaction. Long hours and expectations to work overtime week after week had taken their toll, and with a couple of young children Hai wanted to find a career that would allow him extra time to spend with his kids. Even though the financial security provided by his job was comforting, the importance of building strong family relationships was also important.

Hai decided to enroll in night classes offered at the local community college. He wasn't sure of a particular career direction to follow, but he knew that he wanted a change. He recognized that by going back to school he'd be able to explore new careers and complete the necessary steps that would make a career change possible.

Hai and I met so that I could assist him in the beginning stages of the career exploration process. Personality, interest, and ability tests that he completed confirmed his prior expectation that a career in either a math or science-related field would be appropriate. Hai had always enjoyed math and science classes in high school, and, although he hadn't attended college before, he had maintained his interest in science and math. He mentioned, for example, that he had been an avid member of several computer clubs in his community over the years and had developed a special interest in the Internet. He also recalled that classes requiring some type of computer work had been his favorite.

When we began to explore Hai's work-related values and how they had affected his career choices, Hai asked me what values had to do with jobs and careers. I explained that values are like the cement that binds our career interests and skills together.

For two weeks, Hai engaged in a thorough evaluation of his work-related values and began to realize that he valued job environments that maximized the opportunity for self-directed work activities. He recognized, also, that a job that provided an opportunity to be creative would correspond with his work-related values.

After additional exploration, Hai decided to major in computer science. He began exploring career opportunities in private consulting as well as contract work in computer programming because such options seemed to afford him the independence and freedom that he valued so highly.

Values are the cement that binds our career interests and skills together.

Work-related values, those things about our work environment that matter a great deal to us, are certainly associated with our on-the-job performance and our career-related success. Now is the time for you to begin to consider which types of work-related values you possess. Exercise 4.1, What Makes Work Fun For You?, will help you recognize how your particular values are associated with different types of work environments.

WHAT MAKES WORK FUN FOR YOU?

A. Think about a past job experience you've had that you especially liked. What aspects of the job did you enjoy the most? Below are several different work-related values associated with different types of careers. As you read through the list, decide which work-related factors have helped make jobs satisfying to you in the past or that you believe will contribute to job satisfaction in the future. Remember to complete this exercise based on what work-related values you possess, not what values you think you should possess or what others (e.g., parents, siblings, friends) tell you that you should value.

Circle those work-related factors that you place a high value on:

A particular salary
Location of work
Benefits (e.g., health insurance, retirement plan)
Stable employment
Challenging work responsibilities
Opportunities for advancement/promotion
Opportunities to receive recognition for what you do
Opportunities to develop new skills
Opportunities for variety in your work
Opportunities to travel
Opportunities to work with tools and machines
Opportunities to comfort other people
Opportunities to educate or advise others
Opportunities to be creative
Opportunities to work independently
Opportunities to encourage and motivate others
Opportunities to engage in risk-taking, adventurous behavior
Opportunities to supervise the work of others
Opportunities to be systematic and organized in your work
Opportunities to assist others less fortunate than you
Opportunities to participate in innovative projects
Opportunities to hold a position of high visibility
Opportunities to work with other people
Opportunities to influence or persuade others
Opportunities to entertain others

B. The above list is far from comprehensive. List below any other aspects of the work environment that you highly value in a career.

1. _____
2. _____
3. _____
4. _____
5. _____
6. _____
7. _____

C. Now rank the work-related values that you circled in Part A and the additional work-related values listed in Part B in the order of their importance to you. In other words, as you look over the work-related values you circled in Part A and those you included in Part B, write in the value that is the most important to you on the first line below. On the second line, write in the item that to you is the second most important work-related value, and so on—until you've listed all of those qualities that you circled in Part A and included in Part B. The least important values will be at the end of your list.

Most Important _____

_____

_____

_____

_____

_____

_____

_____

_____

_____

_____

_____

Least Important _____

We'll be reviewing this list of work-related values later on in the career decision-making process.

CORE LIFE VALUES

When we talk about work-related values, we're usually referring to those aspects of the work environment that we're likely to experience on the job on a fairly regular basis. Whether our particular occupation provides flexibility in work hours or the opportunity to interact with others or requires out-of-town travel: These are examples of the types of work-related characteristics that we usually examine when integrating values into our career decision.

Core life values are the principles and beliefs that make you who you are.

As you continue with the career decision-making process, however, consider other values you possess, and think about how they might influence your career satisfaction and success. I call these other, more personal values, *core life values*. Core life values differ from work-related values in that they are all-encompassing. They represent the things in life that matter to you the most, the principles and beliefs that make you who you are.

The best example I have to illustrate the importance of core life values in career decision making comes from my own experience as a student. Toward the end of my senior year, one of the decisions I had to make was whether to pursue a graduate degree. I was on my way to completing a bachelor's degree in psychology, and thoughts of entering a graduate program in counseling had crossed my mind. However, I was already employed on a part-time basis as a producer at a large radio station in Los Angeles, and for several years I was set on pursuing a career in radio.

I visited a career counselor, and we worked together for several weeks. I completed the MBTI and an interest inventory; then we discussed my skills and abilities in a variety of domains and reviewed some of the experiences I had enjoyed during high school and college. The results of the inventories and our discussions confirmed that both careers (radio broadcasting *and* counseling) seemed to be in line with my personality, interests, abilities, and experiences. I had a fair amount of interest in both options, I had demonstrated skills in both areas, and I had enjoyable experiences in both fields.

I was beginning to think that I might as well toss a coin in the air to decide my career choice. That's when the counselor asked me to think about my values. I followed my counselor's advice and generated a list of core life values, those things that I strongly believe in and that matter to me most. I especially considered the role that my cultural background played in the development of my values. My Italian-American heritage and my lower-middle class upbringing certainly influenced my value system. I vividly recall that the first thing I put down on a sheet of paper later that night was the word "family." I went on to generate a list of seven or eight other core life values that matter a great deal to me, but it was that first one I listed, family, that had an important influence on my career decision.

Because I had taken the time to consider those things in life that mattered most, I began to realize that a career as a counselor and university professor would be much more likely to allow me extra time for a spouse and children than would a career in the entertainment industry. The flexibility of work hours associated with operating a private practice or with teaching at a university seemed much more in line with some of my core values than the long hours associated with a career in radio broadcasting. That realization helped me make a career decision that I've been extremely satisfied with ever since.

Personality, interests, abilities, and experiences are certainly important to consider in their own right, but gaining increased awareness of values and understanding their role in career development cannot be overlooked if you want to make career decisions that count. Exercise 4.2, Getting at the Core: What Matters Most?, will help you to think about your core life values as you begin to consider their role in your career development.

4.2　GETTING AT THE CORE: WHAT MATTERS MOST?

In Exercise 4.1, we focused on work-related values, those values that are important to you in an actual occupation or career. Now we turn our attention to your core life values, those values that describe what you stand for in life.

A.　Begin by generating a list of the core values that you most strongly believe in. Allow yourself some time to think about what values are most important to you in life and why. Be sure to consider the ways that your cultural and ethnic background, gender, age, and social class have influenced your value system.

Don't expect to be able to complete this exercise in a minute or two. The more thought you give to this exercise, the more successful you'll be at integrating your values into the career decision-making process. Remember, your core life values may not seem related to career decision making at this point, but you'll begin to see their connection as you continue the exploration process.

To help you get started, the following sampling of some core life values are provided for your reference. Feel free to include these and any other values that you consider to be important in your list.

Achievement	Fame
Adventure	Family relationships
Availability to my children	Financial comfort
Availability to my spouse or significant other	Freedom
Church participation	Friendships
Community outreach	Generosity
Education	Health
Environment	Honesty
Ethics	Independence
Integrity	Recognition
Intellectual stimulation	Religion
Leisure time	Respect
Loyalty	Safety
Material wealth	Security
Patriotism	Sense of accomplishment
Personal appearance	Social status
Physical fitness	Spiritual development
Power	Time to myself

My Core Life Values

Value: _____

Why It Is Important to Me

_____

_____

_____

_____

Value: _____

Why It Is Important to Me

_____

_____

_____

_____

Value: _____

Why It Is Important to Me

_____

_____

_____

_____

Value: _____

Why It Is Important to Me

_____

_____

_____

_____

Value: _____

Why It Is Important to Me

_____

_____

_____

_____

Value: _____

Why It Is Important to Me

_____

_____

_____

_____

Value: _____

Why It Is Important to Me

_____

_____

_____

_____

Value: _____

Why It Is Important to Me

_____

_____

_____

_____

B. Now review your list of core life values and rank order them based on their importance to you. The value that is most important to you should be listed on the first line below, and the remainder of your core values should follow in order, just as in Exercise 4.1.

Most Important _____

_____

_____

_____

_____

_____

_____

_____

_____

_____

_____

Least Important _____

Chapter 8 discusses the ways that your values can be integrated with other information you've been gathering about yourself. But first we will begin the process of narrowing down your career options in Chapters 5, 6, and 7.

Integrating Information About Yourself

This chapter will help you begin to narrow your list of career possibilities to those that most closely match your personality, interests, abilities, and experiences. In many ways, it's the core chapter of the book, the chapter in which most of your hard work and dedication to the career decision-making process will begin to pay off. This is the chapter that ties it all together.

In Chapter 1 you were introduced to the world of work and to some of the important issues you should consider when making career decisions. In Chapter 1 you began storing information about different careers and work projections in general so that the information would be available to you at a later time in the career decision-making process.

In Chapter 2, you were introduced to Dr. Super's theory of career development and the five stages of the career decision-making process, including growth, exploration, establishment, maintenance, and disengagement. In Chapters 3 and 4, we examined the importance of personality, interests, abilities, experiences, and values

when making career decisions. You completed several assessments designed to assist you in increasing your awareness of what makes you a unique individual and of how those qualities are associated with various work environments.

Now that you've completed the exercises in Chapters 3 and 4, you're probably beginning to get a better sense of what Dr. Super meant by the term self-concept, and why one of his core ideas is the importance of maximizing your chances to implement your self-concept. Your own, personal understanding of who you are—of your likes and dislikes, your skills and weaknesses, your experiences and values—is what determines your self-concept. You are the best judge of what you enjoy doing and, as such, are the world's greatest expert when it comes to making your own career decisions.

The primary purpose of this chapter is to help you integrate information about your personality, interests, abilities, and experiences so that you'll be better prepared to make important career decisions. In particular, you'll learn some helpful ways to evaluate your responses to the exercises in Chapter 3 as you begin to narrow your career choice possibilities. You'll also select four or five particular careers that you can explore in more depth in the chapters that follow.

MATCHING SELF-CONCEPTS WITH WORK ENVIRONMENTS

Our career satisfaction and stability and on-the-job performance depend on congruence, or the match between our self-concept and our work environment.

As you may recall from Chapter 1, Dr. Anne Roe characterizes work environments as consisting of eight different types: Service, Business Contact, Organization, Technology, Outdoors, Science, General Culture, and Arts and Entertainment. A summary of Dr. Roe's model is shown in Table 5.1.

Like many other career counselors and psychologists, Dr. Roe believes that our career satisfaction and success are directly related to the match between our self-concept and our work environment. Dr. John Holland, a world-renowned vocational psychologist mentioned in Chapter 1, refers to this match as the person-environment fit, or *congruence*. Dr. Holland believes that individuals with high levels of congruence will be more satisfied with their careers, achieve greater success within their occupations, and will remain in their careers over a relatively long period of time. Persons with low levels of congruence, on the other hand, are likely to experience job dissatisfaction and relatively poor on-the-job performance and are likely to search for new career directions that might be more satisfying.

To illustrate this concept let's turn to an example that I witnessed at the very beginning of my career. One of the first students I worked with, Chandra, was a senior attending a college on the West Coast. Chandra was about to graduate with a degree in mechanical engineering, and she talked about the many challenges she faced during her college years.

Throughout her first year in college, Chandra found that she struggled a great deal when it came to writing assignments of various sorts. She had a very hard time preparing research papers and found it extremely difficult to answer essay questions on tests. She just couldn't seem to get her thoughts down on paper very easily.

In her sophomore year Chandra had discovered that she had a learning disability. After thoughtful planning with the Director of Special Student Services on campus, Chandra had been able to work though the challenges posed by her disability. She took advantage of the tutoring services available at the university and worked with her instructors to make sure appropriate accommodations were available to her in each of her classes. As a result, Chandra was able to overcome the

Summary of work environments.   **table 5.1**

WORK ENVIRONMENT	SAMPLE OCCUPATIONS	CHARACTERISTICS OF PEOPLE WHO LIKE WORKING IN THESE ENVIRONMENTS
Service	Social worker Marriage counselor Police officer Occupational therapist	Enjoy serving and attending to the personal tastes, needs, and welfare of other people; obtain a strong sense of satisfaction from helping and/or protecting other people.
Business Contact	Real estate agent Salesperson Insurance agent Public relations specialist	Enjoy persuading other people to engage in a particular course of action, such as the purchase of a commodity or service.
Organization	Employment manager Accountant Business executive Small-business owner	Enjoy engaging in tasks that involve a high level of organization and precision; often satisfied by supervising or managing others.
Technology	Electrical engineer Mechanic Truck driver Carpenter	Enjoy producing, transporting, and/or fixing things; more satisfied working with tools and objects than with people.
Outdoors	Gardener Wildlife specialist Farmer Horticulturalist	Enjoy working in outdoor settings; often favor working with animals and plants rather than with people.
Science	Chiropractor X-ray technician Dentist Paleontologist	Enjoy working with scientific theory and its application to real-world problems.
General Culture	Lawyer High school teacher Librarian Historian	Enjoy interacting with groups of people in an effort to preserve and/or transmit knowledge and cultural heritage.
Arts and Entertainment	Interior decorator Professional athlete Choreographer Art teacher	Enjoy environments that provide opportunities for artistic expression and/or the use of special skills in an entertainment industry.

challenges posed by her disability and performed very well in her more demanding engineering courses.

Despite the appearance that all was well, however, Chandra was not looking forward to graduation, and in fact was anxious and fearful about beginning her career as an engineer. As we explored possible reasons for her feelings, it became apparent that Chandra's anxieties were due to one simple fact that she had only recently realized: she didn't like engineering! After four years of classes and some part-time work in the industry, Chandra had recognized that a career in engineering was probably not such a good idea after all.

As Chandra discussed her situation with me I was reminded of how important it is to engage in career development activities early on in one's college years. I worked with Chandra to help her clarify the reasons engineering was probably not as appealing as she thought it would be. I asked her to explain the work environment of an engineer to me, and then I asked her to describe the types of activities that she liked, the range of abilities that she had, and the things that mattered most to her in life. It didn't take long for us to realize why a career in engineering didn't excite Chandra at this point in her life.

Chandra had prepared for a career in a field best characterized in Dr. Roe's classification system as a technical working environment. As a mechanical engineer, Chandra would be working with her hands a great deal, in a routine, organized setting with relatively little face-to-face contact with other people. Yet based on her self-concept, her understanding of her personality, her likes and interests, her skills and talents, and her values and beliefs, it was clear that Chandra was likely to be much more satisfied working in a service environment.

She loved to be around large groups of people. She enjoyed the opportunity to teach others and help them find solutions to their problems. She preferred working with people rather than with things, and she placed a high value on work that provided lots of opportunity to interact with others. For Chandra, a career as a mechanical engineer wasn't a very good match between self-concept and work environment. According to Dr. Roe's theory, a career associated with social service would probably be much more fulfilling for her. Consequently, Chandra began to explore careers such as social work and counseling.

The challenge is to seek career opportunities that will maximize your chances of establishing a high level of congruence between your personality, interests, and skills and your work environment. Developing a strong self-concept comes from thinking about how your personality, interests, abilities, experiences, and values all interact with one another. Now it's time to pull that information together and integrate the results of the exercises you completed in Chapter 3 in hopes of determining which of the work environments are most likely to produce career satisfaction, stability, and success for you.

For many of us, brief descriptions of the eight work environments (such as those provided in Table 5.1) are all we really need in order to make a pretty good guess about which types of careers would provide the best match for us. But assessments similar to those that we completed back in Chapters 3 and 4 provide additional information that almost always helps increase the reliability of our decisions.

You may find that the results of the assessments confirm what you had already suspected. Or you may discover that the exercises helped you recognize aspects of yourself that you weren't aware of before. Either way, completing Exercise 5.1, Finding Your Career Type, will help increase your awareness of your self-concept and enhance your ability to select the best type of work environment for you.

FINDING YOUR WORK ENVIRONMENT **5.1**

Begin by scoring the exercises that you completed in Chapter 3. To complete this process, remove the pages in Appendix B and then turn back to the appropriate pages in Chapter 3.

For each of the Chapter 3 exercises that you score, you will have a point value corresponding to each of the eight career types. Fill in those values in the spaces below.

Scores from Exercise 3.1

Service	Business Contact	Organization	Technology	Outdoors	Science	General Culture	Arts and Entertainment
___	___	___	___	___	___	___	___

Scores from Exercise 3.2

Service	Business Contact	Organization	Technology	Outdoors	Science	General Culture	Arts and Entertainment
___	___	___	___	___	___	___	___

Scores from Exercise 3.3

Service	Business Contact	Organization	Technology	Outdoors	Science	General Culture	Arts and Entertainment
___	___	___	___	___	___	___	___

Scores from Exercise 3.4

Service	Business Contact	Organization	Technology	Outdoors	Science	General Culture	Arts and Entertainment
___	___	___	___	___	___	___	___

Scores from Exercise 3.5

Service	Business Contact	Organization	Technology	Outdoors	Science	General Culture	Arts and Entertainment
___	___	___	___	___	___	___	___

Total Scores (add each of the scores in the columns above)

Service	Business Contact	Organization	Technology	Outdoors	Science	General Culture	Arts and Entertainment
___	___	___	___	___	___	___	___

Once you've recorded your scores from each of the exercises in Chapter 3, compute your total scores in each area by summing the responses for each type.

Since the TOTAL SCORES are the combined results from the assessments you completed to evaluate your personality, interests, skills, and experiences, they can be used to help you determine your self-concept as it relates to career and work environments. Your primary "career type" is the category for which your score is the highest. Your secondary career type is the category for which your score is the second highest. Your third level of career type would be the category for which your score is the third highest. If the scores for two of your types are identical, then your career type is probably best described as a combination of those two types.

Write in the three occupational types for which your total scores were the highest:

1. _____

2. _____

3. _____

DISCOVERING CAREERS THAT MATCH CAREER TYPES

Now that you have a good idea what your primary career type is, it might be helpful for you to take a look at careers that are congruent with your self-concept. Begin this process by skimming through the occupational lists located in Appendix C. Most interest inventories include lists of occupations for you to consider with regard to your career type.

As you review the lists, make a note of those careers that interest you the most. There will be many careers listed that are simply not interesting to you even though they are listed as congruent with your career type. That's certainly to be expected. But, at the same time, you're likely to find that many of the careers congruent with your type are rather interesting and, therefore, worthy of continued exploration.

If your primary career type as revealed in Exercise 5.1 is several points higher than any of the other types, then it probably only makes sense to take a look at occupations that correspond with your primary type. If, however, the results of Exercise 5.1 revealed primary and secondary career types whose point totals were rather close to one another, then you might want to take a look at the careers listed in all three categories you listed.

exercise **5.2** FINDING INTERESTING CAREERS FOR YOUR CAREER TYPE

Make a list below of all those careers for which you have at least some degree of interest in pursuing further, either now or at some later time. Don't limit yourself only to careers listed in Appendix C or in some other list of occupations made available to you; instead, include *any* careers you think that you could realistically pursue.

List of Interesting Careers

_____

_____

_____

_____

_____

_____

_____

_____

Now comes the tough part. In order to complete some of the exercises that follow in the remaining chapters, you need to narrow your list of potential career options to the four or five that interest you the most. For some folks, this is a rather easy task, but for others it can be much more difficult. The following case studies are provided to show you how you can use the information you've gathered up to this point to help you make more informed career choices.

CASE STUDIES IN NARROWING CAREER OPTIONS

consider Mario & Meredith

As you've done in previous chapters, Mario, a first-year college student, completed several assessments of his work-related interests and skills. A review of his results indicated primarily an Arts and Entertainment career type, which helped to confirm his own hunch. He consulted Appendix C for a listing of occupations corresponding to the Arts and Entertainment work environment. Many of the careers that Mario found listed in the Appendix were ones that he had thought about at different times throughout his life, but now he had a much better sense of his work-related and core life values.

Mario knew that he wanted to pursue a career that would provide a chance for creative expression and some degree of autonomy, but he also wanted a career that would provide a stable income. He had an actor friend who often went four or five months without work, and that simply wasn't something Mario was willing to do: He wanted to make sure he was getting a regular paycheck. Although his longer list of career possibilities included occupations such as freelance artist and actor, Mario selected careers in interior design and commercial art to pursue in more detail.

Meredith's situation was somewhat different than Mario's; she had a difficult time even generating a list of initial career options. She couldn't recall ever having been set on one type of career. She had taken lots of different classes in college, but none of them seemed to stand out as any more interesting than the others.

The results of Meredith's interest and ability tests helped her to understand why she was having such a difficult time narrowing down career options: Her primary and secondary career types were nearly identical in value. When she completed Exercise 5.2, she discovered that Arts and Entertainment and Service career types were only two points different from one another. In essence, Meredith's career interests included both components equally.

When it came time to look through lists of careers, Meredith took a look at both the Arts and Entertainment and Service occupation groupings. What resulted was a list of 18 occupations that she thought might be worth pursuing further. She went from wondering whether she would find any careers fulfilling to the other extreme—making a list of many careers she might like to pursue. When I explained to her that she needed to narrow the list down to four or five, she thought about the educational requirements associated with each career.

Meredith had two young children and was a single mother. She didn't want to select a career that would require several years of graduate school—at least not for an entry-level position. That helped her narrow her list down a bit as did her consideration of the earning potential of each of the jobs. Her resulting list of career options included social worker, art teacher, and addictions counselor.

Whether your situation is like Mario's, Meredith's, or is something else altogether, the information you've been gathering about the world of work and the increased awareness you have about your self-concept will help you a great deal as you narrow your list of potential careers down to four or five.

Think about pursuing those careers that will be congruent with your values.

Perhaps the most important things for you to re-evaluate at this time are your work-related and core life values. As you make this initial step to narrow your list of potential career options, it's very important that you think about pursuing those careers that will be congruent with your values. If you're like most people, you certainly don't want to engage in a thorough exploration of a career that you know is going to conflict with many of your work and life values. Reviewing Exercises 4.1 and 4.2 (pages 41–42 and 44–46) will help you make better, more informed career decisions and prepare you for Exercise 5.3, Narrowing Your Career Options.

NARROWING YOUR CAREER OPTIONS

Based on the information that you've gathered up to this point, and based on the preliminary career choices you made earlier, now you can narrow your list down to the four or five career options that seem most worthy of continued exploration. Remember to think about the results of all of the research you've been engaging in. What have you learned from those sources of information? How do your values seem supported and challenged in various careers? These are the kinds of questions you want to answer as you create your list.

Now is the time! List the four or five career options that you've decided you'd like to explore in more depth as you continue the career decision-making process.

Career Options

1. _____

2. _____

3. _____

4. _____

5. _____

We'll be referring to this "short list" of career options in subsequent chapters as we learn about specific techniques for exploring potential careers.

6

Methods of Career Exploration

Now that you've identified several occupations that you'd like to learn more about, it's time to begin an active search for a specific career direction. In this chapter, you'll learn various ways to determine which of the occupations you're currently thinking about are worthy of continued consideration. You'll be reminded of important concepts of career exploration presented earlier in the book. You'll also learn about effective techniques for obtaining important employment-related information. The primary goal of this chapter is to assist you in the process of narrowing down your list of potential career options as you continue to work on implementing your self-concept.

A REVIEW OF THE CAREER EXPLORATION PROCESS

You may recall from Chapter 2 that Dr. Super referred to the second phase of the career decision-making process as exploration. In Chapters 3, 4, and 5 you engaged in activities related to the crystallizing stage of exploration. You began by thinking about some of your career dreams and childhood aspirations. Then you considered the importance of integrating your self-concept when making career choices.

You have now completed exercises designed to increase your understanding and awareness of your personality, interests, experiences, and values, and you have been shown how each of these areas influences your career decision-making behavior. At the end of Chapter 5 you were able to consider various factors that helped narrow your original list of career options down to four or five.

Now it's time to embark on the specifying substage of career exploration and make some of the most critical decisions about whether to pursue particular careers. Each exercise completed during this stage will require you to do some important research about the careers you're considering.

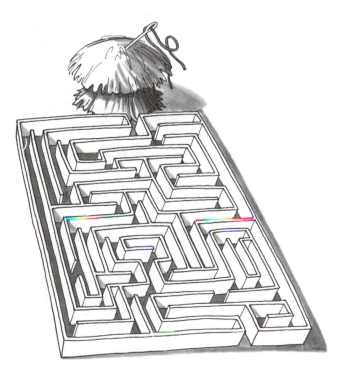

DEVELOPING AN ORGANIZED SYSTEM OF INFORMATION GATHERING

Create a file for each of the occupations on your narrowed "short list" of career possibilities.

The first and most important activity that you'll be engaging in during this stage of career development is information gathering. In Chapter 1 you were encouraged to begin collecting and organizing materials from books, magazines, newspapers, and other sources that you might find particularly useful. You were also reminded about the information that student service groups, clubs, and organizations can provide.

If you haven't already done so, create a separate file for each of the occupations that you included in your occupations list at the end of Chapter 5. Throughout the next couple of weeks, you'll be collecting important information about these careers and including that information in your occupation files.

GATHERING INFORMATION ABOUT CAREERS

There are many sources available to you for learning more about the careers you're interested in. This section will show you how each of these sources can provide information that should be considered when making career decisions.

Get to know your reference librarians.

You'll greatly benefit from getting to know your library's reference librarians. Many of the sources you'll want to consult as you explore various career options are available in public and university libraries. The more comfortable you are working with the reference librarians, the more likely you'll be to use this priceless resource of guidance and information. Simply put: Get to know your reference librarians.

U. S. Department of Labor Publications

Occupational Outlook Handbook

As mentioned in Chapter 1, the *Occupational Outlook Handbook* is published every two years by the U. S. Department of Labor's Bureau of Labor Statistics. Hundreds of occupations are included in each issue of the handbook. For each occupation that is listed, the *Occupational Outlook Handbook* provides a description of the nature of the work, general working conditions, expected earnings, educational and training qualifications, opportunities for advancement, and a five-year employment outlook. See Figure 6.1 for an example of an entry in the *Handbook*.

The *Handbook* also provides you with a listing of sources that might be helpful for collecting additional information about a particular occupation. The *Handbook* is available at most public libraries as well as college and university libraries and learning centers. Most campus-based career-development and placement centers also keep a current copy on hand.

Occupational Outlook Quarterly

The U. S. Department of Labor's Bureau of Labor Statistics also publishes the *Occupational Outlook Quarterly*. This publication serves as an update to the *Occupational Outlook Handbook*. It includes additional information about several of the jobs listed in the *Handbook*. Because the *Occupational Outlook Handbook* is only published every two years, these quarterly updates can be helpful in obtaining the most accurate information. The quarterly can usually be found at institutions that also subscribe to the *Handbook*.

Sample entry from the *Occupational Outlook Handbook.* **figure 6.1**

Construction and Building Inspectors

(D.O.T. 168.167-030, -034, -038, -046, and -050; .267-010, -102; 182.267; 850.387, .467)

Nature of the Work

Construction and building inspectors examine the construction, alteration, or repair of buildings, highways and streets, sewer and water systems, dams, bridges, and other structures to ensure compliance with building codes and ordinances, zoning regulations, and contract specifications. Inspectors generally specialize in one particular type of construction work or construction trade, such as electrical work or plumbing. They make an initial inspection during the first phase of construction, and follow-up inspections throughout the construction project to monitor compliance with regulations. In areas where severe natural disasters—such as earthquakes or hurricanes—are more common, inspectors monitor compliance with additional safety regulations.

Building inspectors inspect the structural quality and general safety of buildings. Some specialize—for example, in structural steel or reinforced concrete structures. Before construction begins, *plan examiners* determine whether the plans for the building or other structure comply with building code regulations and are suited to the engineering and environmental demands of the building site. Inspectors visit the work site before the foundation is poured to inspect the soil condition and positioning and depth of the footings. Later they return to the site to inspect the foundation after it has been completed. The size and type of structure and the rate of completion determine the number of other site visits they must make. Upon completion of the entire project, they make a final comprehensive inspection.

A primary concern of building inspectors is fire safety. They inspect structure's fire sprinklers, alarms, and smoke control systems, as well as fire doors and exits. In addition, inspectors may calculate fire insurance rates by assessing the type of construction, building contents, adequacy of fire protection equipment, and risks posed by adjoining buildings.

Electrical inspectors inspect the installation of electrical systems and equipment to ensure that they function properly and comply with electrical codes and standards. They visit work sites to inspect new and existing wiring, lighting, sound and security systems, motors, and generating equipment. They also inspect the installation of the electrical wiring for heating and air-conditioning systems, appliances, and other components.

Elevator inspectors examine lifting and conveying devices such as elevators, escalators, moving sidewalks, lifts and hoists, inclined railways, ski lifts, and amusement rides.

Mechanical inspectors inspect the installation of the mechanical components of commercial kitchen appliances, heating and air-conditioning equipment, gasoline and butane tanks, gas and oil piping, and gas-fired and oil-fired appliances. Some specialize in inspecting boilers or ventilating equipment as well.

Plumbing inspectors examine plumbing systems, including private disposal systems, water supply and distribution systems, plumbing fixtures and traps, and drain, waste, and vent lines.

Public works inspectors ensure that Federal, State, and local government construction of water and sewer systems, highways, streets, bridges, and dams conforms to detailed contract specifications. They inspect excavation and fill operations, the placement of forms for concrete, concrete mixing and pouring, asphalt paving, and grading operations. They record the work and materials used so that contract payments can be calculated. Public works inspectors may specialize in highways, structural steel, reinforced concrete, or ditches. Others specialize in dredging operations required for bridges and dams or for harbors.

Home inspectors conduct inspections of newly built homes to check that they meet all regulatory requirements. Home inspectors are also increasingly hired by prospective home buyers to inspect and report on the condition of a home's major systems, components, and structure. Typically, home inspectors are hired either immediately prior to a purchase offer on a home or as a contingency to a sales contract.

Construction and building inspectors increasingly use computers to help them monitor the status of construction inspection activities and keep track of permits issued. Details about construction projects, building and occupancy permits, and other documentation are now generally stored on computers so that they can easily be retrieved and kept accurate and up to date.

Although inspections are primarily visual, inspectors often use tape measures, survey instruments, metering devices, and test equipment such as concrete strength measurers. They keep a daily log of their work, take photographs, file reports, and, if necessary, act on their findings. For example, construction inspectors notify the construction contractor, superintendent, or supervisor when they discover a code or ordinance violation or something that does not comply with the contract specifications or approved plans. If the problem is not corrected within a reasonable or specified period of time, government inspectors have authority to issue a "stop-work" order.

Many inspectors also investigate construction or alterations being done without proper permits. Violators of permit laws are directed to obtain permits and submit to inspection.

Working Conditions

Construction and building inspectors usually work alone. However, several may be assigned to large, complex projects, particularly because inspectors specialize in different areas of construction. Though they spend considerable time inspecting construction work sites, inspectors may spend much of their time in a field office reviewing blueprints, answering letters or telephone calls, writing reports, and scheduling inspections.

Inspection sites are dirty and may be cluttered with tools, materials, or debris. Inspectors may have to climb ladders or many flights of stairs, or may have to crawl around in tight spaces. Although their work is not considered hazardous, inspectors usually wear "hard hats" for safety.

Inspectors normally work regular hours. However, if an accident occurs at a construction site, inspectors must respond immediately and may work additional hours to complete their report.

Nearly 60 percent of all construction and building inspectors work for local governments.

(continued)

figure 6.1 Continued.

Employment

Construction and building inspectors held about 64,000 jobs in 1994. Over 50 percent worked for local governments, primarily municipal or county building departments. Employment of local government inspectors is concentrated in cities and in suburban areas undergoing rapid growth. Local governments employ large inspection staffs, including many plan examiners or inspectors who specialize in structural steel, reinforced concrete, boiler, electrical, and elevator inspection.

About 18 percent of all construction and building inspectors worked for engineering and architectural services firms, conducting inspections for a fee or on a contract basis. Most of the remaining inspectors were employed by the Federal and State governments. Many construction inspectors employed by the Federal Government work for the U.S. Army Corps of Engineers or the General Services Administration. Other Federal employers include the Tennessee Valley Authority and the Departments of Agriculture, Housing and Urban Development, and Interior.

Training, Other Qualifications, and Advancement

Individuals who want to become construction and building inspectors should have a thorough knowledge of construction materials and practices in either a general area, like structural or heavy construction, or in a specialized area, such as electrical or plumbing systems, reinforced concrete, or structural steel. Construction or building inspectors need several years of experience as a manager, supervisor, or craft worker before becoming inspectors. Many inspectors have previously worked as carpenters, electricians, plumbers, or pipefitters.

Employers prefer to hire inspectors who have formal training as well as experience. Employers look for persons who have studied engineering or architecture, or who have a degree from a community or junior college, with courses in construction technology, blueprint reading, mathematics, and building inspection. Courses in drafting, algebra, geometry, and English are also useful. Most employers require inspectors to have a high school diploma or equivalent even when they qualify on the basis of experience.

Certification can enhance an inspector's opportunities for employment and advancement to more responsible positions. Most States and cities actually require some type of certification for employment. To become certified, inspectors with substantial experience and education must pass stringent examinations on code requirements, construction techniques, and materials. Many categories of certification are awarded for inspectors and plan examiners in a variety of disciplines, including the designation "CBO," Certified Building Official. (Organizations that administer certification programs are listed below in the section on Sources of Additional Information.)

Construction and building inspectors must be in good physical condition in order to walk and climb about construction sites. They also must have a driver's license. In addition, Federal, State, and many local governments may require that inspectors pass a civil service examination.

Construction and building inspectors usually receive most of their training on the job. At first, working with an experienced inspector, they learn about inspection techniques; codes, ordinances, and regulations; contract specifications; and record keeping and reporting duties. They usually begin by inspecting less complex types of construction, such as residential buildings, and then progress to more difficult assignments. An engineering or architectural degree is often required for advancement to supervisory positions.

Because they advise builders and the general public on building codes, construction practices, and technical developments, construction and building inspectors must keep abreast of changes in these areas. Many employers provide formal training programs to broaden inspectors' knowledge of construction materials, practices, and techniques. Inspectors who work for small agencies or firms that do not conduct training programs can expand their knowledge and upgrade their skills by attending State-sponsored training programs, by taking college or correspondence courses, or by attending seminars sponsored by the organizations that certify inspectors.

Job Outlook

Employment of construction and building inspectors is expected to grow faster than the average for all occupations through the year 2005. Growing concern for public safety and improvements in the quality of construction should continue to stimulate demand for construction and building inspectors. Despite the expected employment growth, most job openings will arise from the need to replace inspectors who transfer to other occupations or who leave the labor force. Replacement needs are relatively high because construction and building inspectors tend to be older, more experienced workers who have spent years working in other occupations.

Opportunities to become a construction and building inspector should be best for highly experienced supervisors and craft workers who have some college education, some engineering or architectural training, or who are certified as inspectors or plan examiners. Thorough knowledge of construction practices and skills in areas such as reading and evaluating blueprints and plans are essential. Governments—particularly Federal and State—should continue to contract out inspection work to engineering, architectural and management services firms as their budgets remain tight. However, the volume of real estate transactions will increase as the population grows, and greater emphasis on home inspections should result in rapid growth in employment of home inspectors. Inspectors are involved in all phases of construction, including maintenance and repair work, and are therefore less likely to lose jobs during recessionary periods when new construction slows.

Earnings

The median annual salary of construction and building inspectors was $32,300 in 1994. The middle 50 percent earned between $25,200 and $43,800. The lowest 10 percent earned less than $19,400 and the highest 10 percent earned more than $57,500 a year. Generally, building inspectors, including plan examiners, earn the highest salaries. Salaries in large metropolitan areas are substantially higher than those in small local jurisdictions.

Related Occupations

Construction and building inspectors combine a knowledge of construction principles and law with an ability to coordinate data, diagnose problems, and communicate with people. Workers in other occupations using a similar combination of skills include drafters, estimators, industrial engineering technicians, surveyors, architects, and construction contractors and managers.

Sources of Additional Information

Information about a career and certification as a construction or building inspector is available from the following model code organizations:

☛International Conference of Building Officials, 5360 Workman Mill Rd., Whittier, CA 90601-2298.

☛Building Officials and Code Administrators International, Inc., 4051 West Flossmoor Rd., Country Club Hills, IL 60478.

☛Southern Building Code Congress International, Inc., 900 Montclair Rd., Birmingham, AL 35213.

Information about a career as a home inspector is available from:

☛American Society of Home Inspectors, Inc., 85 West Algonquin Rd., Arlington Heights, IL 60005.

For information about a career as a State or local government construction or building inspector, contact your State or local employment service.

Sample entry from the *Dictionary of Occupational Titles.*

figure 6.2

045.107-014 COUNSELOR, NURSES' ASSOCIATION (medical ser.)
Offers vocational, educational, and professional counseling to registered professional nurses, licensed practical nurses, and prospective professional and practical nurse students: Compiles credentials and prepares biographies of counselees. Provides information relative to qualifications required, opportunities for placement and advancement, wages, hours, and other data pertaining to selected field of work to assist nurses in determining educational and vocational objectives. Refers qualified nurses to employers for placement. Assists in establishing personnel policies relative to placement. Aids applicants in obtaining vocational, health, or other assistance from community agencies. May assist in recruitment.
GOE: 10.01.02 STRENGTH: S GED: R5 M4 L5 SVP: 8 DLU: 77

Dictionary of Occupational Titles

The United States Government also publishes the *Dictionary of Occupational Titles* (currently in its fourth edition, revised). The *Dictionary of Occupational Titles* includes descriptions of thousands of different occupational titles as well as a brief definition of each occupation listed and specific information about the skills required for successful performance within that occupation. The *Dictionary* also discusses the types of tasks and materials associated with each occupation, the industries with which the occupation is typically identified, and the working environment. Occupations are arranged alphabetically and by job categories (see Figure 6.2). Like the *Occupational Outlook Handbook*, the *Dictionary of Occupational Titles* is available at most libraries and college career centers. Some sites may have a computer software version available for your use.

Guide to Occupational Exploration

The *Guide to Occupational Exploration* was originally developed as a supplement to the *Dictionary of Occupational Titles.* Details about various occupations are arranged on the basis of interest areas and work environments. This can be a helpful source of information about particular occupations that you might be interested in. The guide is not as widely available as the *Occupational Outlook Handbook* or the *Dictionary of Occupational Titles*, but it may provide you with data you're unable to locate in other sources. If a *Guide for Occupational Exploration* is available to you, it would be worth your time and energy to look through it for useful information.

Additional U. S. Department of Labor Publications

In addition to publishing the *Occupational Outlook Handbook*, *Occupational Outlook Quarterly*, *Dictionary of Occupational Titles*, and *Guide for Occupational Exploration*, the U. S. Department of Labor also sponsors the publication of other useful documents, such as "Job Options for Women" and the "Job Guide for Young Workers." These and other types of publications that address a particular aspect of the world of work may be available at local libraries. If you're unable to locate them, you might want to contact the Bureau of Labor Statistics, U. S. Department of Labor, Washington, D. C. 20212 (202-219-7316). The Bureau's Public Affairs Office will be able to help you obtain useful information relevant to the careers you're pursuing.

Encyclopedia of Careers and Vocational Guidance

The *Encyclopedia of Careers and Vocational Guidance* is similar in many ways to the *Occupational Outlook Handbook*. The encyclopedia is published every few years by the J. G. Ferguson Publishing Company in Chicago and is found in the reference sections of many libraries. The current edition of the *Encyclopedia* is published in four volumes, including separate volumes for industry profiles, professional careers, general and special careers, and technical careers. Information about each occupation listed in the *Encyclopedia* includes details about the history of the career, nature of the work involved, job requirements, employment opportunities, average salaries, and related occupations.

Magazines and General Trade Books

As briefly discussed in Chapter 1, there are many magazines and general trade books that may also help you locate information about occupations. Probably the best way to determine what information is available about a particular topic is to use an index system available at nearly every library.

The *Periodical Guide to Literature* can be used to locate articles in newspapers and magazines that may provide you with helpful insights about an occupation. The *Periodical Guide* is published every month and has an updated listing of articles arranged by general topic area. If you're researching information about occupational trends in accounting, for example, you would look up "Accounting" in the *Periodical Guide*. Below that term would be a reference list of articles and magazines for which accounting is the main topic of interest. You could then scan the abbreviated list of titles to determine which sources would be worth your time to obtain.

Some magazines that you might consider reading on a regular basis so that you can get a good idea of general employment and labor trends include *Business Week*, *Forbes*, *Fortune*, and *Inc.* The rule of thumb is to keep your eye out for any material that may help you gain a better understanding of the world of work and the occupations for which you are seeking additional information. Be sure to consult magazines and books that are especially relevant to your life situation. There are many publications specific to persons of certain ethnic and racial backgrounds, women, or persons with disabilities.

Many libraries these days also have computerized search systems that can be helpful for finding books on a particular topic. Again, if you're interested in accounting careers, you would follow the instructions for the particular system you're using and probably type the word "accounting" at some point along the way. The system would then provide you with books available at that library (or other libraries in the system) that deal with accounting issues.

Several other indexes may be available to you. Some of the more helpful index systems include *Occupational Abstracts*, *Sociological Abstracts*, and *Educational Resources in Circulation (ERIC)*. Check with reference librarians to find out what sources they're aware of that can help you locate information about occupations.

Newspapers

Many of the newspapers with large circulations, such as the *Los Angeles Times* or the *Washington Post*, often cover the labor market and employment projections on a fairly regular basis. The *Wall Street Journal* is another reliable source of information about the world of work. However, as mentioned earlier, don't forget about your local newspaper. The most accurate information about local and regional trends in the job market is more likely to be found in your local newspaper than anywhere else.

College and University Career Centers

If you're currently attending college, don't forget to check out the services offered by your own institution. Most colleges and universities offer a wide variety of career exploration services. In addition to offering many of the sources discussed in this chapter, career development centers usually have established networks for linking you up with community businesses that can be especially valuable during your job search. Career counselors can also be valuable resources for getting you in touch with appropriate support services on campus that may assist you throughout the career exploration process.

Informational Videos

Videotapes can be another useful source of information about various careers. Individuals who are currently working in certain fields are often interviewed for documentary-type videos, and important information about occupations is usually provided. Informational videos can be especially helpful in giving you an idea of what job settings might be like on a day-to-day basis. These types of videotapes are often available from a career center or school library or from an institution's media center.

Computerized Career Information Programs

One of the best ways to locate information about occupations is to learn about and use computerized career programs available in college and university career centers. The more popular programs include the System of Interactive Guidance and Information (SIGIplus), Computerized Heuristic Occupational Information and Career Exploration System (CHOICES), and DISCOVER.

Computerized career information delivery systems can provide you with up-to-date information about occupations as well as provide you with additional assessments of your interests and skills. Most of the systems also include accurate details about training and educational opportunities associated with certain occupations as well as updated descriptions much like those found in the *Dictionary of Occupational Titles* and the *Occupational Outlook Handbook*.

The Internet and the World Wide Web

As mentioned in Chapter 1, one of the fastest growing methods for finding out about occupational trends and for gathering specific occupational information is the Internet. For information about how to use the Internet in your career exploration, you might consult your career center or your teacher. Also, bookstores and libraries have books that specifically cover using the Internet in job exploration.

Various Internet sites are designed to support career exploration and job search strategies of specific groups. For example, sites exist for some ethnic groups, students with disabilities, students returning to college after many years away from school, and homemakers who have decided to pursue another career.

Informational Interviewing

After you have used the print and electronic media to research careers, you will benefit greatly from interviewing people who are already employed in occupations you're considering. Informational interviewing may be one of the most direct sources of information you can use.

A primary source for informational interviews is people you already know. Think about whether anyone you know is already working in a career you're considering—or whether your acquaintances know someone else in the field. You could also try using your local telephone directory to contact persons who are working in careers you're considering.

> ### *Informational Interviewing:*
> ### *Questions to Ask About a Potential Career*
>
> - What interested you in this career?
> - What preparation did you need for obtaining this job?
> - What do you like most about your career?
> - What do you like least about your career?
> - What are your job responsibilities?
> - What stress do you experience on the job?
> - What personal qualities are important in your work?
> - What are the prospects for someone entering your line of work today?
> - Is this field expanding? In what ways is it changing?
> - What is the salary range for a person in this field?
> - What are the opportunities for promotion?
> - If you were to give advice to someone considering this career, what would it be?
> - Are there any other sources of information about this career that you are aware of?

Be aware that some of the people you call may not even have 5 or 10 minutes to speak with you. Don't get discouraged. You'll probably be rather surprised at the number of people currently working in a career area who will actually jump at the opportunity to talk with someone interested in pursuing the same career that they have pursued.

An important first step to this process is setting up the initial appointment. When you introduce yourself to potential interviewees, be sure to explain that you are in the process of exploring different career options and that you would like to spend a few minutes talking with them about their chosen career. You might want to let them know a little bit about your background and why you're considering a career in their field of expertise.

If possible, make an interview appointment at the individual's place of business. This is not only more convenient for the person you interview, but it also gives you an opportunity to experience the work environment of the career you are considering.

Informational interviewing is not job interviewing. When you interview for a job, someone asks you questions. When you interview for information about a career, *you* ask the questions. See the accompanying box, "Informational Interviewing: Questions to Ask About a Potential Career," for the types of information you may want to obtain from an informational interview.

Helen, a student I worked with a few years ago, discovered the value of informational interviewing as she explored various career options. Helen had been a homemaker for many years. Her youngest child was in fourth grade, and she wanted to return to the workforce. Helen's husband was very supportive of her decision to go back to work and encouraged her to meet with a career counselor to explore the possibilities. She was particularly interested in pursuing a career that directly involved helping others. She was also looking forward to going back to school for the education that helped to secure such work.

After meeting with me for a couple of months, Helen narrowed down her list of career options to nursing, teaching, and counseling. The information she gathered from traditional sources, such as the *Occupational Outlook Handbook* and the *Guide to Occupational Exploration*, was somewhat helpful, but she was still having a difficult time figuring out which career would be best to pursue. Then we discussed the idea of interviewing current nurses, teachers, and counselors, and Helen agreed that such an activity might be a good one.

By talking with current nurses in the area, Helen discovered that there were shortages in nearly every nursing field. Helen was leaning toward psychiatric nursing, one of the specialties for which there was a particular need. Discussions with teachers and counselors in her community revealed the opposite situation in those occupational fields. Teachers mentioned how difficult it was to find a job in the local market, and counselors described their difficulty in finding and maintaining a client base large enough to stay in business. This information was extremely valuable to Helen as she considered the importance of locating employment in her own community.

Helen eventually decided to obtain a nursing license. When I last spoke with her, she was in her second year of school at a local community college and well on her way to a career that is very likely to bring her satisfaction and enjoyment.

Indeed, informational interviews are often helpful sources in career exploration. Don't forget to utilize this option when seeking additional information about the occupations you're considering.

Career Fairs

Many high schools and colleges sponsor annual career fairs. These are usually day-long events that provide you with the opportunity to learn more about specific occupations and find out about actual employment options in your community. Some cities sponsor career fairs for members of their community who are not able to attend school-based functions. Career fairs can be especially helpful if you're still considering several careers and want to learn about current hiring trends and practices.

State Employment Service

Many states operate an employment service (sometimes referred to as the state unemployment office) that can be of great assistance to you throughout the career exploration process. You may even be fortunate enough to live close to a local office of your state's employment service or in a state that provides computerized access to employment information. It would be beneficial for you to contact the service for a variety of reasons. State employment services often have access to information regarding statewide job trends and projections. They can also be a valuable source of information about local training options that are available. If you're unable to locate a local service center, call your state representative or the state government office in your area to inquire about this service.

Community Leaders

Another way to get information about job trends in your geographic region is to contact some of the leaders in your community. Chambers of commerce and other business organizations and clubs can provide you with helpful information as well as networking opportunities. Getting to know business and community leaders can also prove essential to securing employment. Try to make some of these valuable contacts as you continue the career exploration process.

Friends and Family

Countless clients have reminded me over the years that friends and family members can be sources of helpful information about occupations. As you begin narrowing down your employment options, it'll be important to get feedback from those who know you best.

National Career Development Association

The National Career Development Association is a national organization of career counselors and professionals who are interested in career development issues. The association is affiliated with the American Counseling Association and is headquartered in Alexandria, Virginia.

Each year the National Career Development Association compiles a listing of current career literature that you may find helpful as you explore various career options. The list is published each summer in the association's journal, *The Career Development Quarterly.* The materials that are included in the list will provide you with information about particular job categories and occupations. Names and addresses of publishers of the materials are listed in the journal so that you can access them. Information about the journal and other publications sponsored by the National Career Development Association can be obtained by contacting the Executive Director of the Association, 5999 Stevenson Avenue, Alexandria, VA 22304, (800) 347-6647.

Local Trade Associations and Unions

Another way to gather accurate information about various occupations is to contact local trade associations and unions in your area. They'll be glad to provide you with information about local job trends, working conditions, and projected employment opportunities.

Jerry, a recent client, was interested in a career as a plumber. He obtained some information from the *Occupational Outlook Handbook* and found several recently published articles in newspapers and magazines on employment trends in the plumbing industry, but the information that he found most helpful was provided by the local plumbers union. Union representatives sent Jerry several documents that explained how to become an apprentice in the area, a required step to becoming a member of the local plumbers union. Jerry was able to secure an apprenticeship within a month after receiving the material, and he is now a member of the local union.

Exercise 6.1, The Career Information Form, will help you pull together the occupational information you gather over time.

Throughout this chapter you've been introduced to various sources available to you for gathering important information about occupations. Let's put that information into a consistent format so that you can make career decisions a little more easily.

6.1 THE CAREER INFORMATION FORM

Three copies of the Career Information Form in this exercise are included at the end of the chapter. Make extra copies as needed so that you can complete the exercise for each of the careers you're considering.

Write in the occupations (in the space provided at the top of each form) that you'd like to learn more about. You might want to look back at the list you generated at the end of Chapter 5. Using the various sources of information discussed in this chapter, try to find answers to as many of the questions about each occupation as possible.

Don't get discouraged if it takes a little time to complete this project. You may have to consult several different sources before finding out all of the information for each occupation, but remember that the career decisions you'll be making are going to directly influence many aspects of your life. Devoting a substantial amount of time and energy to this process is well worth the investment.

To give you an idea of how you might go about completing these forms, a sample is provided. The information to complete the sample form was obtained from several sources, including the *Occupational Outlook Handbook*, the *Dictionary of Occupational Titles (D.O.T.)*, the *Encyclopedia of Careers and Vocational Guidance*, a few newspaper articles, current employees in the airline industry, the state employment service, and DISCOVER (one of the computerized career information systems mentioned earlier).

A Sample Career Information Form

GENERAL INFORMATION

Title of Occupation: _____ Flight Attendant _____

D.O.T. #: _____ 352.367-010 _____   Roe's Occupational Type: _____ Service _____

NATURE OF WORK

General Working Conditions:

Flight attendants work for airline companies and have duties both on the ground and in the air.

Employee Responsibilities:

The primary responsibility of a flight attendant is to ensure that passengers have a safe, comfortable, and enjoyable flight. They perform a variety of pre-flight and in-flight tasks. They attend briefing sessions of the flight crew prior to takeoff, check supplies and safety equipment, welcome passengers, attend to their needs, serve food and drinks, and carry out some clerical duties.

Physical Demands:

Flight attendants carry out the majority of their duties on their feet. Most airlines, therefore, require that employees pass a physical exam. Many airlines require that eyesight be at least 20/50 if not corrected and 20/20 with eyeglasses or contacts.

Potential Work Hazards:

The most obvious potential work hazard is the possibility of a flight-related emergency (e.g., malfunctioning equipment, dangerous weather). Flight attendants are not classified, however, as working in a particularly hazardous occupation.

Worker Characteristics:

The most successful flight attendants are described as being congenial, pleasant, poised, tactful, and resourceful. Flight attendants who seem to enjoy their job most are those who have a desire to serve the public, think clearly and logically, and don't mind following instructions.

Degree of Worker Independence:

Flight attendants usually work in a team atmosphere, although smaller aircraft often require only one flight attendant on board each flight. Most flight attendants enjoy working with coworkers.

General Pros and Cons to Employment:

For a family-minded person, regular travel away from home might be problematic. The salary is usually not as high as it might be in other occupations. At the same time, travel for a flight attendant and her or his family members is nearly free, and there are many opportunities to see other parts of the world.

EMPLOYMENT TRENDS AND PROJECTIONS

Current Supply and Demand for Workers:

According to the information I gathered, there's always a much larger public interest in flight attendant work than there are jobs available. Many people try for years to become a flight attendant and still aren't selected for an interview.

Future Prospects:

According to the *Occupational Outlook Handbook*, there will probably be a greater increase in flight attendant positions over the next 5 to 10 years compared to many other careers. This doesn't mean, however, that obtaining jobs will get any easier; there will still be keen competition. If I could obtain two years of college and get some experience working with the public, I would greatly increase my chances of being hired.

Stability of Employment:

Turnover rates are very low these days. Most people who become flight attendants hold on to their jobs for many years.

Opportunities for Advancement:

There are a number of possibilities for advancement: first flight attendant (purser), supervising flight attendant, instructor, recruitment representative, and chief attendant. As in most industries, obtaining advanced positions is competitive.

QUALIFICATIONS

General Qualifications for Employment:

The ability to follow directions and a pleasant personality are important in this field.

Educational/Training Requirements:

At least a high school diploma (although some college is helpful) and completion of a flight training school are required.

Minimum Aptitude:

Knowledge of emergency procedures and of flight regulations and procedures is required.

Preparation Standards:

Some college is helpful; completion of a couple of years of college will increase chances of being hired. Four to six weeks in intensive flight training school are required once hired on.

WORKLOAD AND SALARY INFORMATION

Typical Hours Worked Each Week/Month:

This usually varies from 55 to 85 hours of actual flight time each month. There are also several hours each week during which flight attendants are away from home if their employment happens to require layovers (most positions do).

Salary Range:

Between $13,000 and $40,000. The average salary for a flight attendant who has worked about 6 years is around $20,000.

Benefits:

Expenses (food, transportation, housing) paid for while on duty. Paid sick leave and vacation time. Travel is virtually free for flight attendants and their families. Some companies offer additional benefits, too (such as life insurance).

RELATED OCCUPATIONS

Several different kinds of occupations are related to aspects of the flight attendant job, including firefighter, camp counselor, emergency medical technician, host/hostess, and safety consultant.

SOURCES OF ADDITIONAL INFORMATION

Future Aviation Professionals of America
4959 Massachusetts Boulevard
Atlanta, GA 30337
1-800-JET-JOBS

Association of Flight Attendants
1625 Massachusetts Avenue, NW
3rd Floor
Washington, DC 20036

JOB SHADOWING

In addition to gathering the types of information needed to complete Exercise 6.1, another effective method that will help you narrow down your career options is job shadowing. Job shadowing refers to a hands-on exercise in which you learn about many of the day-to-day tasks and responsibilities associated with occupations you're considering. When you job shadow, you actually follow someone around (as if you were their shadow) as they engage in the various duties associated with their job.

Job shadowing teaches you about the day-to-day responsibilities of the jobs you're considering.

The benefits of job shadowing are numerous. Not only will you be able to get a first-hand sense of what employment in particular careers is really all about, but you might also have the opportunity to make some important job contacts that could come in handy in the future.

Samantha, a young woman I once worked with, expected to have a very rough time breaking into the male dominated field of carpentry. She had a strong interest in carpentry as a profession, but was afraid she might be discriminated against because of her gender. During exploration of this career option, I encouraged Samantha to job shadow with a local carpenter in town.

After the job shadowing experience, Samantha became even more committed to pursuing a career in carpentry. Furthermore, the person who Samantha "shadowed" ended up offering her summer employment with his company and eventually a full-time position. By taking the time to engage in job shadowing, Samantha not only had the opportunity to see what type of work a carpenter did on a daily basis, but she reaped the benefit of obtaining an actual job that she might not have otherwise even applied for.

Exercise 6.2, Job Shadowing, will help you prepare for and evaluate your job shadowing experiences.

JOB SHADOWING

A. First, decide which occupations you'd like to job shadow. Based on the results of the previous exercise, you may have already begun the process of narrowing down your list of preferred occupations. If you haven't made some definite decisions to remove one or more of those occupations from further consideration, then you should probably consider job shadowing each occupation you listed at the end of Chapter 5.

List below those occupations that you'd like to job shadow:

1. _____

2. _____

3. _____

4. _____

5. _____

B.   The next step is to contact individuals who are currently working in the occupational areas you've listed. Most of the sources described in this chapter can provide you with helpful information in this regard. You'll probably have the best results in locating someone to talk with by using the telephone directory, contacting local community leaders, checking with trade organizations and associations, and asking friends and family members for some contacts. Local offices of the state employment service might also be able to help you with this task.

When arranging for a job shadow experience, keep in mind that you'll find a great deal of variety in the opportunities that are available to you. You might only be able to spend a couple of hours in some locations, while other businesses might invite you to spend a day or even a whole week observing the work that goes on there.

Try to get in contact with the company's chief human resources director if you don't already know an employee you can observe on the job. The human resources director will probably be able to provide you with general information regarding job shadowing as well as put you in contact with particular employees you could work with. Don't assume that the person you talk with is going to know automatically what "job shadowing" is all about. Explain that you're in the process of making some career decisions and that you'd like to observe the work that goes on in their setting for a few hours to get a better idea of the day-to-day activities associated with that career.

It might be a good idea to job shadow the same occupation a couple of different times, with employees from different companies or organizations. You probably won't be making any definitive conclusions about a career based solely on job shadowing, but with only one shadowing experience, you risk getting a biased view of that career.

C.   You'll have the opportunity during the job shadowing exercise to observe a variety of things about the nature of a career. Pay especially close attention to those details that are likely to influence your decision of whether or not to continue pursuing a career in that particular industry. Take a look at the Job Shadow Evaluation Form that follows before engaging in the activity to get an idea of some of the important questions you should be thinking about during the exercise.

D.   Make as many copies of the Job Shadow Evaluation Form as you need. After each of your job shadowing experiences, use one copy of the form to evaluate the occupation. As you complete the forms, focus on information you learned from the experience that you were not aware of prior to job shadowing. You'll be using this information to assist you in the narrowing down process in Chapter 8.

Job Shadow Evaluation Form

Title of Occupation: _____

D.O.T. #: _____   Roe's Occupational Type: _____

Job Shadow Date and Time: _____

Business Name: _____

Address: _____

Contact Person: _____   Phone: _____

General Working Conditions:

Tasks and Duties:

Things I Learned About That I Didn't Already Know:

Overall Impressions of the Job:

THE VALUE OF PART-TIME AND VOLUNTEER EXPERIENCES

Part-time or volunteer work is a useful method of gathering information about careers.

Perhaps the most comprehensive method for gathering information about potential careers is to obtain actual part-time or volunteer work experience. Working with high school and college students over the years, I've been constantly reminded that one of the best ways to learn about a career is to obtain on-the-job experience. Although it may not always be easy to identify part-time or volunteer work that's available in the career fields you're interested in, you may be surprised about how many opportunities actually exist for you to obtain such experiences.

If you discover that obtaining part-time work in careers you're considering is unlikely, then you might at least try getting some experience in a field that's related to your career interests. Someone who is considering a career as a financial planner, for example, may not find any jobs or volunteer experiences in financial planning per se, but there may be other part-time opportunities available that are related to financial planning. Work as a bank teller or tax assistant might at least provide such a person with the chance to see what occupations related to financial management are all about.

Working part-time or volunteering in a career you're exploring will allow you to see if it's really the right career for you. You'll be able to determine, long before you've completed all of the necessary educational and training requirements, whether that particular career is worth continued pursuit.

Michael, a student I worked with a few years ago, is a perfect example of how obtaining valuable part-time work experience can be beneficial during career exploration. Michael was fairly confident that a career as a gerontological counselor (a counselor who works with the elderly) was the best career choice for him, and all indications from the assessments and inventories Michael completed seemed to support his decision.

Michael grew up in a poverty-stricken neighborhood in the Southwest and spent a lot of his time as a young man caring for his grandparents and many of the other older citizens in his community. He explained to me that he was rather confident that he wanted a career, such as gerontological counseling, that would provide him with the opportunity to work with older people on a regular basis.

A few months after we began working together, Michael was fortunate enough to find a volunteer position working at a local nursing home. A couple of weeks later, I asked Michael how working at the nursing home was going, and he responded that he wasn't having much fun at all. He explained that working with the elderly was very different than he thought it would be. Michael still wanted to pursue a career in the helping professions, but he had learned—based directly on his volunteer experience—that working with the elderly was not the best option for him after all. When you realize that preparation for a career as a gerontological counselor includes the completion of a bachelor's degree followed by at least two years of graduate school and about a year of internship placement within a gerontological setting, you begin to see the value of Michael's having obtained some part-time experience early in his education. If he had waited until his internship experience during graduate school, Michael may have found himself in an all-too-common situation: having prepared for a career that isn't as rewarding as originally thought.

Many academic departments at colleges and universities have established relationships with different companies and organizations within the community that may have opportunities available to you. Career centers on most college campuses offer a variety of internship and cooperative learning activities that may be able to provide you with similar experiences. Connections you may have through a religious or community service organization might also help you identify potential sites for obtaining volunteer work experience associated with your career options. Appendix D provides a brief overview of several job search strategies that you might find helpful as you search for part-time or volunteer job openings.

Methods of Information Gathering for Career Exploration

Reference Librarians

Can assist you in locating information related to your career options and organizing your information search

U.S. Department of Labor Publications

- *Occupational Outlook Handbook*
- *Occupational Outlook Quarterly*
- *Dictionary of Occupational Titles*
- *Guide to Occupational Exploration*
- Additional publications relevant to certain populations and careers

Encyclopedia of Careers and Vocational Guidance

Contains information about an occupation's history, the nature of work involved, job requirements, employment opportunities, average salaries, and related occupations

Magazines and General Trade Books

Includes a variety of publications that provide career-specific information and general employment trends

Newspapers

Provide you with national and local information about certain employment trends and projections

College and University Career Centers

Offer a wide variety of career-exploration and job-search services

Informational Videos

Helpful for giving you an idea of what job settings are like on a day-to-day basis

Computerized Career Information Programs

Include systems such as SIGIplus, DISCOVER, and CHOICES, which provide you with up-to-date information about occupations and additional assessments of your personality, interests, skills, and values that can be integrated into your career decisions

(continued)

*Methods of Information Gathering
for Career Exploration,* continued

The Internet and the World Wide Web

Provide access to information about occupational trends and specific occupations as well as job openings across the country

Informational Interviewing

Involves identifying and interviewing individuals working in various careers in your community

Career Fairs

Provide you with the opportunity to learn about specific occupations and find out about actual employment options in your area

State Employment Service

Provides access to information regarding statewide job opportunities and trends

Community Leaders

Can provide you with helpful information and potential networking opportunities

Friends and Family

Might have information about certain careers you're considering or whom to contact to find out more about them

National Career Development Association

Compiles lists of current career literature that may be helpful to you

Local Trade Associations and Unions

Able to provide you with local employment trends, working conditions, and projected employment opportunities

Job Shadowing

Involves spending time with individuals currently employed in a career you're considering, to learn more about that career option from direct observation

Part-Time and Volunteer Experiences

Allow you the opportunity to "try out" various career options by gaining on-the-job experience

Career Information Form

GENERAL INFORMATION

Title of Occupation: _____

D.O.T. #: _____ Roe's Occupational Type: _____

NATURE OF WORK

General Working Conditions:

Employee Responsibilities:

Physical Demands:

Worker Characteristics:

Potential Work Hazards:

Degree of Worker Independence:

General Pros and Cons to Employment:

EMPLOYMENT TRENDS AND PROJECTIONS
Current Supply and Demand for Workers:

Future Prospects:

Stability of Employment:

Opportunities for Advancement:

QUALIFICATIONS
General Qualifications for Employment:

Educational/Training Requirements:

Minimum Aptitude:

Preparation Standards:

WORKLOAD AND SALARY INFORMATION
Typical Hours Worked Each Week/Month:

Salary Range:

Benefits:

RELATED OCCUPATIONS

SOURCES OF ADDITIONAL INFORMATION

Career Information Form

GENERAL INFORMATION

Title of Occupation: _____

D.O.T. #: _____ Roe's Occupational Type: _____

NATURE OF WORK
General Working Conditions:

Employee Responsibilities:

Physical Demands:

Worker Characteristics:

Potential Work Hazards:

Degree of Worker Independence:

General Pros and Cons to Employment:

EMPLOYMENT TRENDS AND PROJECTIONS
Current Supply and Demand for Workers:

Future Prospects:

Stability of Employment:

Opportunities for Advancement:

QUALIFICATIONS
General Qualifications for Employment:

Educational/Training Requirements:

Minimum Aptitude:

Preparation Standards:

WORKLOAD AND SALARY INFORMATION
Typical Hours Worked Each Week/Month:

Salary Range:

Benefits:

RELATED OCCUPATIONS

SOURCES OF ADDITIONAL INFORMATION

Career Information Form

GENERAL INFORMATION

Title of Occupation: _____

D.O.T. #: _____   Roe's Occupational Type: _____

NATURE OF WORK

General Working Conditions:

Employee Responsibilities:

Physical Demands:

Worker Characteristics:

Potential Work Hazards:

Degree of Worker Independence:

General Pros and Cons to Employment:

EMPLOYMENT TRENDS AND PROJECTIONS
Current Supply and Demand for Workers:

Future Prospects:

Stability of Employment:

Opportunities for Advancement:

QUALIFICATIONS
General Qualifications for Employment:

Educational/Training Requirements:

Minimum Aptitude:

Preparation Standards:

WORKLOAD AND SALARY INFORMATION
Typical Hours Worked Each Week/Month:

Salary Range:

Benefits:

RELATED OCCUPATIONS

SOURCES OF ADDITIONAL INFORMATION

7

Identifying and Overcoming the Barriers

As you begin to narrow down your career options, it'll be increasingly important for you to think about your chances of achieving your various career goals. One of the best ways to engage in that process is to consider potential barriers that may interfere with your career development and to develop strategies to help you overcome many of these barriers.

The primary purpose of this chapter is to introduce you to the types of barriers that could interfere with your chances of success in the careers you're exploring. You'll learn about the differences between internal and external barriers as well as real versus perceived barriers. Several case studies will be presented to help you gain a clearer understanding of the roles that barriers play in the career decision-making process. You'll also have the opportunity to develop an understanding of specific barriers that may influence your career decisions and to develop strategies to overcome those barriers.

THE ROLE OF BARRIERS IN CAREER DECISION MAKING

For many years now, career counselors have recognized the role that barriers play in the career decision-making process. Barriers are those obstacles that may deter you from reaching a particular career goal. Whether the information we have about particular barriers is accurate or not, we often compromise our career goals based on the barriers we perceive. If we believe that a certain career is not possible because of certain barriers, then we might compromise our goals and begin to consider alternative career options. But recognizing that there are barriers to achieving our career goals doesn't always have to lead to compromise. The more we're aware of potential barriers, the more likely we are to be prepared when we actually face them in the future. This process usually begins by understanding the different types of barriers that can and often do exist in the career decision-making process.

Internal barriers come from inside of us, whereas external barriers come from sources outside of us.

Many of the barriers that influence our career decisions are referred to as *internal* barriers. These are barriers that come from inside of us. We usually have a fair amount of control over internal barriers and, through hard work and effort, can often overcome them. Low levels of confidence in your ability to complete a degree, procrastination, poor study habits, the fear of failure, and concerns about juggling multiple life roles are just a few examples of internal barriers. Such barriers are very real and are clearly very important in the career decision-making process.

Other kinds of career-related barriers are referred to as *external* barriers. These are barriers that come from sources outside of us. We usually have very little, if any, control over these barriers. Global economic trends, educational requirements associated with a particular career, job discrimination, and job availability are examples of external barriers. Although we have a more difficult time controlling external barriers, there are many ways that identifying such barriers can help us achieve our career goals.

Some examples of internal and external barriers that many of us experience in our lives are listed in the box, Examples of Internal and External Barriers. Although this listing of barriers is certainly not all-encompassing, it does provide you with an idea of the differences between internal and external barriers, a distinction that may be helpful to you as you consider the kinds of barriers associated with some of your career interests.

Many people consider various aspects of their cultural background to be potential barriers to career development. Sometimes a person will view her racial background, gender, sexual orientation, religious beliefs, socioeconomic status, or physical disability as a barrier to career success. These factors can be perceived as especially problematic if you expect them to lead to discrimination and prejudice on the job. The important thing to remember is that countless resources exist to help you overcome these and many other barriers.

Examples of Internal and External Barriers

Internal Barriers

Anxiety associated with making career decisions

Concerns about multiple life roles and responsibilities

Fear of failure

Lack of information about a career

Low confidence in your ability to obtain a particular degree

Low self-esteem

Poor study skills

Procrastination

External Barriers

Economic trends

Educational requirements

Financial hardship

Job availability

Job discrimination

Lack of employment contacts

Social hindrances

In terms of employment discrimination on the basis of age, gender, racial and ethnic background, religious orientation, sexual preference, and physical disability, you need to remember that discrimination in *any* form is illegal. Employers are required to hire people on the basis of their qualifications, not their age, gender, race, religion, sexual preference, or physical disability. Still, you may find it useful to contact labor organizations in your area that can offer support in your efforts to secure a career in a particular field. If you have any doubt regarding your treatment in an employment setting, contact the Equal Employment Opportunity/Affirmative Action office in your community.

Persons with disabilities, both physical and mental in nature, often wonder how they'll be able to engage in certain kinds of work given their particular disability. Knowledge about available resources is a key factor to overcoming these potential barriers.

The Americans with Disabilities Act (ADA), passed in 1990, protects all individuals from job discrimination on the basis of disabilities (which covers all physiological conditions affecting one or more of the body's systems as well as mental and psychological disorders). Visual, hearing, and speech impairments, cerebral palsy, epilepsy, muscular dystrophy, multiple sclerosis, HIV, cancer, diabetes, emotional illness, and learning disabilities are just a few of the types of disabilities protected under the law.

In her book, *Job Strategies for People with Disabilities*, Melanie Witt explains that prospective employers must provide "reasonable accommodations" to employees who have a disability of some sort. These types of accommodations can range from making a building more accessible to offering variable work hours to employees with special needs. Special equipment might be purchased or changes in the work environment might be made to help employees complete their tasks more efficiently.

Most college and universities have someone who is responsible for assisting students with disabilities in all aspects of their educational and career development. The Dean of Students office would be able to direct you to the appropriate resources on your campus. To find out more about the types of services available to persons with disabilities in your state, contact the state government office responsible for ensuring compliance with ADA regulations. You might also want to contact the Department of Justice, Office for ADA Information, P.O. Box 66118, Washington, DC 20035. The ADA Hotline is (202) 514-0301.

REAL VERSUS PERCEIVED BARRIERS

As you begin to think about the kinds of barriers that are relevant to your life situation, you'll need to be able to distinguish between *real* and *perceived* barriers.

Gloria, a student I worked with, had decided that she was going to go back to school to pursue a degree in criminal justice. Gloria was in her late forties, and her two children were grown and living on their own. Gloria had always thought about returning to school to become qualified to work in law enforcement. With more free time on her hands, Gloria decided to begin to make that dream a reality.

Like many people who return to the world of work after several years away from the scene, Gloria was starting to wonder if she really had what it takes to succeed in an academic training program. She had made a list of obstacles that she believed were likely to interfere with her career goal. As I reviewed her list of barriers, I began to wonder how accurate Gloria's perceptions were about the obstacles on the list.

One of the barriers Gloria had listed, for example, was weak writing skills. I asked her how she reached that particular conclusion, and she mentioned that it

consider Gloria

had been almost 25 years since she had written a formal paper in school. When I asked her if she had received any recent feedback about her writing skills, she began to realize that her perception wasn't based on actual feedback, but rather on her hunch that she probably had poor written communication skills relative to other college students.

As Gloria and I continued working together, it became increasingly apparent to both of us that many of the barriers she had listed were not really as problematic as she had originally thought. Results of aptitude tests, for example, revealed that Gloria's writing skills were actually above average for college students. The increased awareness that came from our discussion of barriers proved to be very helpful in assisting Gloria to make more informed career decisions.

Sometimes determining whether barriers are real or perceived is a difficult thing to do.

consider Monique

A few years ago I worked with Monique, a 42-year-old Native American woman who was recovering from a stroke. When Monique and I first met, she had narrowed down her career options to legal secretary, medical office receptionist, and preschool teacher. After Monique gathered ample information about these various options, I asked her to think about the types of barriers associated with each potential career direction.

Barriers related to a career as a preschool teacher that Monique identified included her difficulty in engaging in physical activities and the educational requirements associated with such a career. Barriers associated with work as a legal secretary or medical receptionist included the physical pain she experienced when sitting for long periods of time and the problems she had been experiencing with her eyesight. Monique was concerned that she might have some difficulty reading transcripts and other legal documents. Monique was also concerned about her financial situation and its impact on all career options.

There were also many social hindrances that Monique realized could potentially serve as barriers to her career goals. Her parents were both getting rather old and were in need of daily care. Her husband and children were encouraging her to stay home and spend more time recovering from her stroke. Friends were offering their suggestions as to what she should do. Everyone seemed to have an opinion about what was best for Monique. She was clearly aware that her career decision was going to have an impact on the lives of many other people.

After weighing the pros and cons of the various career options, paying especially close attention to the potential barriers associated with each, Monique decided to pursue part-time work as a medical office receptionist, something she had a couple of years experience with prior to her stroke. Taking the time to think about the many different barriers that could influence her satisfaction and success proved to be very helpful to Monique.

Think about the potential barriers that might develop as you continue the career exploration process.

In Chapter 8 you'll be narrowing down your list of career options even further than you have already. But before you make some of those decisions, think about the potential barriers that might develop as you continue to engage in the career exploration process. After developing a list of potential career-related barriers, you'll be able to work on identifying very specific methods for overcoming those barriers.

Identifying barriers is much simpler for some people than it is for others. Many people are already aware of the barriers that stand in their way of reaching the goals they've set for themselves. Others need some help identifying them. Furthermore, many barriers—both internal and external—can seem like insurmountable obstacles.

But identifying specific barriers associated with a career can help you determine what steps you need to take in order to overcome potential obstacles.

A few years ago I worked with Juan, a high school senior who was very interested in a career as a professional athlete. His parents were concerned that by focusing on a career in professional sports, Juan was "ignoring other careers" that he might be more likely to succeed in. Juan was a first-generation college student. In fact, he was the only one in his family ever to graduate from high school. His parents, both of whom came from a low socioeconomic background, wanted to do all that they possibly could to ensure Juan's success.

Consider Juan

I asked Juan to outline his career goals, and, as expected, he explained that he was really only interested in pursuing a career as a professional athlete. When I asked Juan to explain reasons for his interest in professional sports, it became apparent that he enjoyed the outdoors, the ability to engage in competition, and the possibility of earning (as he put it) "a whole lot of money."

I then asked Juan to outline some of the potential barriers that might interfere with his career goal. His initial response was that there really weren't any barriers, no reason at all to think that he wouldn't succeed in professional sports. The way he looked at it, since he had already received numerous awards in high school for his athletic performance, he had no reason to think that professional sports would be any different. My purpose in working with Juan certainly wasn't to persuade him to change his mind about a career in professional sports, nor did I want to decrease Juan's confidence in his abilities. I simply wanted him to recognize that there might be some potential barriers to becoming a professional athlete—just as there are for any career option—that were worth considering.

To assist Juan in the process, I encouraged him to talk with some of his friends and family members to get their feedback about potential barriers associated with a career in professional sports. I also arranged for Juan to interview three professional athletes and talk with them about some of the barriers that they had overcome over the years. After Juan carried out my suggestion, I asked him to develop a list of potential barriers based on what he had learned. As I had hoped, Juan was now able to cite several barriers, both external and internal, that he hadn't really thought about before.

Juan did decide to pursue a career as a professional athlete. The last I heard, he was playing professional baseball for a Triple-A farm club team. After considering all of the potential barriers and establishing ways to overcome many of them, Juan was able to proceed with his career goal with increased knowledge and an awareness of the kinds of challenges he was likely to experience over time.

The experiences of Gloria, Monique, and Juan illustrate why identifying potential barriers to career goals is so important. By exploring perceived barriers, Gloria was able to obtain a more realistic appraisal of her skills. By considering the various internal and external barriers associated with various career options, Monique was able to make an accurate assessment of the best career option for her to pursue at that point in her life. And by identifying possible barriers related to becoming a professional athlete, Juan was better able to prepare to meet the challenges that he encountered along the way.

Exercise 7.1 is designed to help you generate a list of potential barriers associated with the career options you're still considering. It'll be to your benefit to list all of those barriers, internal *and* external, associated with each of your career options. Exercises 7.2 and 7.3 will help you develop strategies for overcoming some of those barriers as you begin clearing the way for the final stages of the career exploration process.

IDENTIFYING CAREER-RELATED BARRIERS

We're best able to identify potential barriers to a particular career goal when we draw on many different sources of information. Of course, you're the best person to determine which barriers are most applicable to your particular life situation. But talking with friends, family members, and other persons in your life who know you well may help you identify a few barriers that might otherwise slip your mind.

All of the information that you've gathered up to this point about the world of work will probably help you identify many of the internal and external barriers associated with the careers that interest you. Consult that information and the people who know you best as you work on developing your lists of barriers. Five sections for the exercise follow (and additional copies may be made as they are needed) so that you may complete a barriers list for each of the career options you're exploring at this time.

Career Option: _____

Internal Barriers

_____

_____

_____

_____

External Barriers

_____

_____

_____

_____

Career Option: _____

Internal Barriers

_____

_____

_____

_____

External Barriers

_____

_____

_____

_____

Career Option: _____

Internal Barriers

_____

_____

_____

_____

External Barriers

_____

_____

_____

_____

Career Option: _____

Internal Barriers

_____

_____

_____

_____

External Barriers

_____

_____

_____

_____

Career Option: _____

Internal Barriers

_____

_____

_____

_____

External Barriers

_____

_____

_____

_____

You'll refer to these lists of barriers later in the chapter as you begin to develop strategies for overcoming them.

CAREER SELF-EFFICACY AND ITS RELATIONSHIP TO BARRIERS

Self-efficacy is an individual's confidence in his or her ability to accomplish a specific task.

The contributions of Dr. Albert Bandura, one of the world's most renowned psychologists, have helped us gain important insights into human behavior. Many of Dr. Bandura's concepts have been especially helpful in the area of career counseling. One of those concepts is Dr. Bandura's notion of self-efficacy.

Self-efficacy is defined as an individual's confidence in his ability to accomplish a specific task. For example, if a 300-pound barbell were sitting on the floor in front of me, and you asked me how confident I was in my ability to dead-lift the barbell on a scale of one (no confidence at all) to five (very high confidence), I would respond by saying "one." My confidence level is very low when it comes to lifting large amounts of weight. Dr. Bandura would say, then, that I have low self-efficacy for lifting the 300-pound barbell. My self-efficacy for lifting a 300-pound barbell is influenced by several different factors, which we will discuss shortly.

This basic concept applies to overcoming barriers that we believe exist for certain careers. If a person isn't very confident in her ability to overcome certain identified barriers, then it would be appropriate to say that the person has low self-efficacy for overcoming the barriers. If, on the other hand, the person believes that she can overcome many potential career barriers without much of a problem, then she would have high self-efficacy for overcoming those barriers.

One of the most interesting things that Dr. Bandura and other researchers have found about self-efficacy is that the likelihood of a person actually completing a particular task is directly linked with her or his self-efficacy associated with that task. To put it another way, if you're confident in your ability to accomplish something, then odds are that you'll be successful at accomplishing it. If, on the other hand, you aren't very confident in your ability to complete some task, then odds are that you'll probably fail at it.

If you're confident in your ability to accomplish something, odds are that you will accomplish it.

Identifying barriers for certain career options is only the beginning of the process. Once you've listed particular barriers related to the careers you're exploring, you need to work on increasing your confidence (or self-efficacy) and your skills for overcoming those barriers. Granted, there may be many barriers (especially external barriers) that simply cannot be overcome. There isn't a whole lot you can do, for example, to overcome problems with the global economy. But there may be a great deal you can do to overcome many of the internal barriers you've listed.

Consider the case of Anna. Anna was an 18-year-old, first-year community college student. She had been diagnosed with multiple sclerosis at the end of her senior year of high school. School work had always been a challenge for Anna, and academic work in college was no exception. Her physical condition was becoming especially challenging, and Anna was beginning to think that because of her disability, obtaining a college degree might not be possible after all.

Instead of giving up, however, Anna decided to contact the Dean of Students on campus to find out if there were any services on campus that could help her. She discovered that there was an Office of Special Student Services that could assist with her educational and career concerns. After meeting with the Director of Special Student Services, Anna realized that many support services were available to empower her to succeed. Her confidence or self-efficacy for obtaining a college degree increased dramatically because she took the time to explore sources of support that were available to her.

Increasing your confidence in your ability to accomplish certain tasks can play an important role in career decision making. This is especially true when it comes to your confidence or self-efficacy for overcoming career-related barriers. Let's take a closer look at Dr. Bandura's concept of self-efficacy.

Dr. Bandura explained that self-efficacy, our confidence in our ability to accomplish something, is based on four factors. In other words, there are four things that contribute to our level of self-efficacy for something.

- *Previous Experiences* (or Performance Accomplishments)
  Those experiences we've had in the past that are directly related to the task we're trying to accomplish

- *Vicarious Learning*
  Learning about our own abilities by watching others who are like us in one way or another

- *Verbal Persuasion*
  The degree to which other people around us persuade or encourage us to accomplish something

- *Physiological Arousal*
  How excited or anxious we might be as we try to accomplish a given task

Increasing your self-efficacy for overcoming career-related barriers can play an important role in career decision making.

To get a better idea of the factors that influence our self-efficacy, let's return to the 300-pound barbell example. In terms of *previous experiences*, I know that I have never been able to dead-lift any more than 220 pounds (and only that much on a *very* good day). Because of these past experiences, I'm fairly sure that I lack the ability to lift a 300-pound barbell. If I had been able to lift 300 pounds in the past, or at least some amount of weight closer to it (say 275 or 280 pounds), then my confidence level for lifting 300 pounds (in other words, my self-efficacy for lifting 300 pounds) would be much higher. Past experiences directly influence our self-efficacy for accomplishing something.

In terms of *vicarious learning*, the second source of information related to our self-efficacy, I've learned from watching many of my friends lift weights that none of our bodies are built like the folks who we know are able to lift 300 pounds. In other words, I've learned vicariously—not from doing it myself but from watching others—that I'm just not likely to be able to lift 300 pounds. Vicarious learning refers to learning about ourselves by watching others around us who are similar to us in one way or another.

In terms of *verbal persuasion*, I don't recall anyone ever trying to *encourage* me to lift 300 pounds. It's no surprise, then, that my self-efficacy for lifting 300 pounds is rather low. Verbal persuasion influences our self-efficacy for accomplishing a task by either encouraging or discouraging us from trying to accomplish it.

The fourth factor that influences our self-efficacy is *physiological arousal*. Psychologists discovered long ago that we tend to perform best when we experience a moderate degree of anxiety or arousal associated with our performance. An actress who experiences just a little bit of anxiety before a performance is probably going to perform better than she would if there wasn't any anxiety at all. Of course, too much anxiety or arousal can be even more detrimental than no anxiety at all. The lesson here is that a little arousal is not a bad thing. What Dr. Bandura and his colleagues have discovered, as you might expect, is that our self-efficacy for accomplishing a given task is related to our physiological arousal.

The degree to which we're physiologically aroused at any given point may not be something that we have a whole lot of control over, but there's a lot we can do to influence the other three sources of self-efficacy. For instance, think about the role that previous experience plays in the development of our self-efficacy expectations. Dr. Bandura has shown us that our level of confidence in our ability to perform some task is directly related to our previous experiences with that task. It only follows, then, that if we have low self-efficacy for overcoming a particular barrier, then we might need to seek new experiences that will allow us the opportunity to try out different ways to overcome that barrier.

Take, for example, my low self-efficacy for lifting a 300-pound barbell. One way that I might be able to increase my self-efficacy for lifting it would be to identify new experiences that might increase my chances of successfully lifting it in the future. If I were to set up some short-term goals, perhaps increasing my weight-lifting ability to dead-lift 240 pounds by the end of this month, 250 pounds by the end of next month, and perhaps 260 pounds the month after that, I just might increase my chances for eventually lifting 300 pounds.

consider Derrick

This process can work for overcoming career-related barriers. I once worked with a student named Derrick, who had identified poor study habits as a career barrier related to his desire to become a pediatrician. Derrick lived in the inner city in a large metropolitan area in the West. He grew up in an impoverished neighborhood and attributed his poor study skills to financial hardship experienced during his early years. He was beginning to think that his past experiences might keep him from realizing his goal of becoming a pediatrician.

After developing a list of new experiences that might help him overcome this barrier, however, Derrick realized that not knowing how to study properly was probably not such a fatal disaster after all. His list of new experiences included setting up an appointment with the study skills advisor at his college to develop a routine study schedule. This provided Derrick with the opportunity to work on his poor study skills through new *performance accomplishments*. Within a few months, Derrick no longer considered his study habits a barrier at all.

Just as identifying new experiences can help you overcome specific barriers, so can learning from others who have successfully overcome similar types of barriers (what Dr. Bandura calls *vicarious learning*). I remember suggesting to Derrick that he meet with some of the senior pre-med students at his college to get their advice on how to best establish effective study skills strategies. He engaged in the process of *vicarious learning* by watching others who had successfully overcome the same barrier in the past.

Even the amount of *verbal persuasion* you receive related to overcoming a particular barrier can change over time. One of the best ways to use *verbal persuasion* to your advantage is by interacting with friends who will support and encourage you to overcome the barriers you've identified. Derrick had a lot of friends, two brothers, a sister, and a proud mother, all of whom were helpful in encouraging and supporting his efforts to alter his study habits.

You may find that you're fairly confident in your ability to overcome most of the barriers you listed in Exercise 7.1. If so, then you're already well on your way to benefiting from the process of identifying career-related barriers. If, however, your confidence level or self-efficacy for overcoming some of those barriers is less than perfect, Exercise 7.2 may be especially helpful to you.

SELF-EFFICACY CHANGE STRATEGIES

Part I.

Go back to Exercise 7.1 and rate your self-efficacy for overcoming the barriers that you listed for each career option. Rate your confidence level on a scale of 1 *(no confidence at all)* to 5 *(complete confidence)*, and write that number in the left margin next to each barrier that you listed. The rating scale shown below might help as a guide.

1	2	3	4	5
no confidence	very little confidence	some confidence	a lot of confidence	complete confidence

Part II.

If your self-efficacy rating for overcoming a barrier is high (4 or 5), then you've probably already identified ways you might overcome that barrier or will have little difficulty identifying methods for overcoming the barrier in the future. But if your confidence rating is low, you might want to work on ways to increase your confidence for overcoming that barrier.

Keep in mind that there are many barriers—especially those that you've listed as external barriers—that you may not be able to overcome. At the same time, however, you might be able to increase your self-efficacy for overcoming many of the internal barriers for which your current confidence level is low.

A. Take a look again at the lists of barriers you supplied in Exercise 7.1 and select five or six of the barriers for which your self-efficacy rating was 2 or lower. Write these barriers down in the spaces provided on the Overcoming Identified Barriers sections that follow. (Make additional copies of this form as needed.)

B. Think about each barrier you've listed and identify *new experiences* that you might seek in order to help you overcome it. This would be similar to Derrick's decision to meet with the college's study skills advisor and to set up a routine study schedule. List new experiences that might help you work on overcoming each barrier in the spaces provided on each form.

C. List ways that you can use *vicarious learning* and *verbal persuasion* to your advantage. Remember that vicarious learning involves discovering ways to overcome barriers by watching and learning from others. Derrick accomplished this aspect of self-efficacy change by learning from the successful experiences of pre-med students at the college. Verbal persuasion techniques that may help you overcome specific barriers might include asking your friends and family members to support you in your efforts (as Derrick did) or seeking the assistance of a counselor or academic advisor for ongoing support.

Overcoming Identified Barriers

Potential Barrier: _____

Ways to Increase Your Self-Efficacy for Overcoming the Barrier:

New Experiences

_____

_____

_____

Vicarious Learning

_____

_____

_____

Verbal Persuasion

_____

_____

_____

Potential Barrier: _____

Ways to Increase Your Self-Efficacy for Overcoming the Barrier:

New Experiences

_____

_____

_____

Vicarious Learning

_____

_____

_____

Verbal Persuasion

_____

_____

_____

Potential Barrier: _____

Ways to Increase Your Self-Efficacy for Overcoming the Barrier:

New Experiences

_____

_____

_____

Vicarious Learning

_____

_____

_____

Verbal Persuasion

_____

_____

_____

Keep in mind that whether or not you'll be successful in overcoming career-related barriers ultimately depends on how diligent you'll be in carrying out some of the plans identified in this exercise. We'll spend some additional time in Chapter 9 identifying specific action strategies that will be useful to you in the pursuit of your career goals.

IDENTIFYING HELPFUL RESOURCES

As previously mentioned, friends and family members can be important sources of encouragement and support, not only as you work on identifying and overcoming career-related barriers but throughout the decision-making process. The social network that your friends and family members provide is often one of the most important—yet often overlooked—sources of support that can help you in your quest to achieve your career goals. In addition to family members and friends, you probably have access to several other individuals who can help you throughout the career decision-making process. These persons might include a career counselor at a college or university, an academic advisor, a favorite teacher, or a recent college graduate.

For each of us, there will be a different list of individuals who can help us throughout the process of making career decisions. Think about the individuals in your life who can serve as part of your social support network, especially as you begin making some critical decisions about your career.

Consider other resources available to you during these latter stages of career decision making also. You've probably realized by now that there are many different resources available to you to help you make the most effective career decisions possible. In Chapter 6, we reviewed over 20 different sources of occupational information. In Chapters 3 and 4, you learned about the many types of assessments you can complete to help you learn more about your personality, interests, skills, abilities, and values. These and many other resources are probably available to you in one form or another. Exercise 7.3 will help you put together a handy list of all resources, including your social support network, that can aid you during the remaining stages of the exploration process.

> *The social network provided by your friends and family members is one of the most important sources of support in achieving your career goals.*

RECOGNIZING RESOURCES

A. Social Support Network

List below the individuals, including friends, family members, and anyone else you are aware of (such as a teacher, advisor, career counselor, or religious leader) who you believe will be helpful to you as you continue the career decision-making process. Below each person's name and telephone number/E-mail address, list the specific ways that person will be able to help you in the process.

Name _____

Phone Number/E-Mail Address _____

Ways This Person Can Help Me

_____

_____

_____

Name _____

Phone Number/E-Mail Address _____

Ways This Person Can Help Me

_____

_____

_____

Name _____

Phone Number/E-Mail Address _____

Ways This Person Can Help Me

_____

_____

_____

Name _____

Phone Number/E-Mail Address _____

Ways This Person Can Help Me

_____

_____

_____

Name _____

Phone Number/E-Mail Address _____

Ways This Person Can Help Me

_____

_____

_____

Name _____

Phone Number/E-Mail Address _____

Ways This Person Can Help Me

_____

_____

_____

Name _____

Phone Number/E-Mail Address _____

Ways This Person Can Help Me

_____

_____

_____

Name _____

Phone Number/E-Mail Address _____

Ways This Person Can Help Me

_____

_____

_____

Name _____

Phone Number/E-Mail Address _____

Ways This Person Can Help Me

_____

_____

_____

B. Additional Resources

List below all other resources (such as a university career planning and placement center or the local public library) that are available to you as you complete the career decision-making process. Again, be sure to list the specific ways that each resource will be helpful to you.

Resource _____

Location _____

Specific Ways That This Resource Will Be Helpful

_____

_____

_____

Resource _____

Location _____

Specific Ways That This Resource Will Be Helpful

_____

_____

_____

Resource _____

Location _____

Specific Ways That This Resource Will Be Helpful

_____

_____

_____

Resource _____

Location _____

Specific Ways That This Resource Will Be Helpful

_____

_____

_____

Resource _____

Location _____

Specific Ways That This Resource Will Be Helpful

_____

_____

_____

Resource _____

Location _____

Specific Ways That This Resource Will Be Helpful

_____

_____

_____

Resource _____

Location _____

Specific Ways That This Resource Will Be Helpful

_____

_____

_____

Resource _____

Location _____

Specific Ways That This Resource Will Be Helpful

_____

_____

_____

Resource _____

Location _____

Specific Ways That This Resource Will Be Helpful

_____

_____

_____

Resource _____

Location _____

Specific Ways That This Resource Will Be Helpful

_____

_____

_____

Resource _____

Location _____

Specific Ways That This Resource Will Be Helpful

_____

_____

_____

8

Making a Tentative Career Decision

In Chapter 2, you read about the complete career decision-making process as conceptualized by Dr. Donald Super. You may recall that the growth stage of career development involves learning about ourselves and the world of work in general. Following the growth stage, the exploration stage of development includes the tasks of crystallizing, specifying, and implementing a career choice.

In Chapters 3 and 4, you completed a series of exercises to help you engage in the exploration stage of career development. You completed assessments of your interests and skills and evaluated your career and life values. You learned how to combine this information to make realistic career decisions in Chapter 5, and in Chapter 6 you learned about the variety of resources available to you for locating important information about potential career options.

In Chapter 7 you examined how barriers in the environment and within yourself can sometimes act as stumbling blocks unless you develop strategies for overcoming them. With all of these tools in your pocket, you are now much more prepared to make some tentative decisions about your career.

TENTATIVE CAREER DECISION MAKING

Dr. Super used the term *tentative* when referring to the types of decisions made during career exploration, perhaps because he recognized that after weeks or even months or years of exploration, we still might change our minds about the career paths we want to follow. After all, this is an extremely important decision.

That's where Dr. Super's concept of recycling comes in. As we'll discuss in more detail in Chapter 10, the career decisions you're making now will not be the very same career decisions you'll make 10, 15, or 20 years from now. We no longer live in a world where career decisions are only made at one point in our lives. In fact, you'll probably make a career change between 5 and 7 times during your adult life. We're always changing and growing. Our interests, our skills and abilities, our experiences, and even our values change over time. As these aspects of our self-concept change, so do our ideas about which types of careers are most suitable.

Career decisions are no longer made at only one point in our lives.

101

Over the next several months (and perhaps the next year or two) you should continue exploring career options that you deem worthy of exploration. A few weeks of focusing on career decision making is not usually sufficient to make thoughtful career decisions. To the contrary, career exploration is a life long process. In this chapter, you'll be asked to select one of the career options you identified back in Chapter 5 as your tentative career choice. We'll look at the steps involved in making effective career decisions so that, as you recycle through the career decision-making process in the future, you'll understand the concepts involved and will be better prepared to make career decisions that count.

I remember one particular individual who came to my office rather frustrated about his career development. Cary was about to turn 50 years old, and I was the third career counselor he had seen since he graduated from high school. He couldn't understand why he hadn't selected the right career yet and expressed embarrassment for not knowing, at age 50, what he wanted to do when he "grew up."

Actually, Cary had been very successful in a couple of different careers. After graduating from college at age 23, he started out in the real-estate business working with his parents. His bachelor's degree in marketing and finance came in handy as he learned about various aspects of real estate.

After working as a real-estate agent for about 12 years, though, Cary found that the job no longer challenged him the way it once had. So, after re-evaluating his career interests and abilities and taking a look at his values, Cary decided to pursue a career as a financial planner. For the first five or six years, Cary experienced all of the things that he had been looking for in a career change. He was challenged in ways that he never had been before. He was working with clients who were interested in what he had to say, and he was enjoying greater financial wealth and the work flexibility he had hoped for. But after a few more years passed, Cary found himself wanting a change yet again.

I posed two key questions to Cary:

- What's wrong with changing careers?
- What's wrong with accepting the fact that your ideal career might actually change over time?

When I asked Cary these questions, he started to realize that his interests, skills, and values had indeed changed over time, and he began to think about how these changes were influencing his career development.

Now, I suggest you consider some similar questions:

- What's wrong with changing your interests?
- What's wrong with developing new abilities and skills that allow you more flexibility in potential job opportunities?
- What's wrong with realizing that your values can and often do change over time?

Changes in one's occupational status and career direction take a great deal of planning and create some degree of stress. That's why career decisions should be thoroughly evaluated before final decisions are made. But there's certainly nothing wrong with exploring new opportunities and allowing yourself the flexibility to make a career change when the time is right.

Think for a moment about all that you've accomplished up to this point in the career decision-making process and read the accompanying box.

When it's all laid out like that, you can see how much work goes into the process of making career decisions. Each of those steps is necessary if you want to make the most effective career decisions that you possibly can. Our task now is to

Summary of Career Decision-Making Tasks You've Accomplished

1. You've discovered that one of the first things you need to do in order to prepare for making career decisions is to increase your understanding of the world of work, including job trends, occupational projections, and the influence of the economy on job opportunities.

2. You've learned ways to classify occupations, focusing on Dr. Roe's method of organizing work environments into eight categories: Service, Business Contact, Organization, Technology, Outdoors, Science, General Culture, and Arts and Entertainment.

3. You've learned methods for organizing information that you collect about the world of work in general and about specific jobs you're interested in.

4. You've recognized the value of mapping out your future and of setting goals.

5. You've been taught the process of lifelong career development as conceptualized by Dr. Donald Super.

6. You've been shown how to determine which stage of the career decision-making process you're in and which tasks will be especially helpful to you as you continue the process.

7. You've completed assessments of your personality, interests, abilities, and values to better understand your self-concept.

8. You've been taught how to integrate your self-concept as completely as possible when making important career decisions.

9. You've learned about a variety of valuable sources available to you for seeking information about potential career options.

10. You've learned about the role that perceived barriers plays in career decision making, and you've developed strategies for overcoming those barriers.

11. You've identified sources of support that can assist you throughout the career decision-making process, including your social support network and other helpful resources available to you.

pull together all of the information you've been gathering and use it to make a tentative career decision from one of the options you identified in Chapter 5. Reconsider your values and think about how they might influence your career satisfaction and success. You'll want to find a way to maximize the match between your values and the career options that you're considering.

PREPARING TO MAKE THE DECISION

The first step of this tentative decision-making process is to gather all of the data about the world of work that you've collected and organized. You'll also want to get out the information that you've been collecting about each of the career options you selected in Chapter 5, and take another look at the results of the inventories you completed in Chapters 3 and 4. Even though the results of those assessments were used to help you make some of your initial career decisions, they're usually helpful to review again at this stage of the process.

Find a large table or desk to use. You're going to need plenty of work space as you complete the Career Analysis System described in Exercise 8.1. The more comfortable the setting, the more effective your work during this stage of the process is going to be.

8.1 CAREER ANALYSIS SYSTEM

Step I.

There is one copy of the Career Analysis Form provided at the end of this Chapter. You'll be asked to make several copies of the form *after you complete Steps I and II* so that you can analyze the various career options you've identified. The sample forms below illustrate the procedure for this exercise.

Sample Career Analysis Form

Specific Career Option: _____			
Factors	Value Points	Career Score	Weighted Value
_____	_____	_____	_____
_____	_____	_____	_____
_____	_____	_____	_____
_____	_____	_____	_____
_____	_____	_____	_____
_____	_____	_____	_____
_____	_____	_____	_____
_____	_____	_____	_____
		Total Career Points:	_____

First list the values, both work-related and other core life values, that you identified in Chapter 4 as important qualities in a career and ranked in order of importance.

Turn back to pp. 42 and 46 for these lists. Copy both lists, the work-related and core life values, in the first column of your Career Analysis Form under the heading Factors, as shown in the example below:

Sample Career Analysis Form

Specific Career Option: _____			
Factors	Value Points	Career Score	Weighted Value
Time with family	_____	_____	_____
Flexible work schedule	_____	_____	_____
Stable income	_____	_____	_____
Chance to help others	_____	_____	_____
Opportunity for promotion	_____	_____	_____
Social interaction	_____	_____	_____
Opportunity to write	_____	_____	_____
Health insurance	_____	_____	_____
Professional atmosphere	_____	_____	_____
		Total Career Points:	_____

Step 2.

Now think about the various factors that you listed in the first column of your Career Analysis Form and assign numerical points to each of those factors. The points that you assign will represent the importance of each factor (or value) to your career goals. Follow these guidelines for assigning numerical values to each factor:

- The points you assign to the factors on your form should total 100 points (no more and no less).
- These points represent the value or the importance that *you* give to each of the factors.
- Do not assign two or more factors the same number of points unless you want them to be equally weighted in your career decision.
- The more points you assign a given factor, the more that factor will become a part of your career decision.

Sample Career Analysis Form

Specific Career Option: _____			
Factors	Value Points	Career Score	Weighted Value
Time with family	30		
Flexible work schedule	15		
Stable income	10		
Chance to help others	10		
Opportunity for promotion	7		
Social interaction	7		
Opportunity to write	7		
Health insurance	7		
Professional atmosphere	7		
(This column should add up to exactly 100 points.)			
Total Career Points:			

Step 3.

Now is the time to make copies of your Career Analysis Form. You'll need it to evaluate all of the careers you're interested in at this time. Make a few extra copies in case you decide to analyze a few other careers of interest as well. At the top of each Career Analysis Form is a place for you to write in the career option that you'll be analyzing on that particular form. Write the options you identified back in Chapter 5 at the top of each form.

Step 4.

Now determine how well each of the career options that you're considering relates to the factors you've identified as important to your career decision. Go through each Career Analysis Form and determine how well each particular career addresses those factors. Place your rating of each factor in the column labeled Career Score, using the following scale:

1	2	3	4	5	6	7	8	9	10

Factor Not Addressed   ⟵·················⟶   Factor Is Completely
by the Career at All   Addressed by the Career

Let's look at an example to illustrate this step. Suppose that one of the career options I had identified for myself back in Chapter 5 was "College Counselor." My Career Analysis Form for College Counselor might look something like this:

Sample Career Analysis Form

Specific Career Option: __College Counseling__			
Factors	Value Points	Career Score	Weighted Value
Time with family	30	8	
Flexible work schedule	15	7	
Stable income	10	9	
Chance to help others	10	10	
Opportunity for promotion	7	9	
Social interaction	7	10	
Opportunity to write	7	6	
Health insurance	7	10	
Professional atmosphere	7	9	
		Total Career Points:	

The career points I assigned to College Counselor reflect my understanding of how well a career as a college counselor meets those factors that I consider critical to my career satisfaction and personal happiness. For example, based on the information that I've gathered, the job shadowing that I've completed, and my understanding of employment opportunities in college counseling, it seems to me that a career as a college counselor would provide a fair amount of time for me to spend with my family. My rating of "8" for the factor labeled "Time with family" reflects my awareness that a career as a college counselor would do a pretty good job meeting that particular need. On the other hand, my rating of "6" for the factor labeled "Opportunity to write" reflects my understanding that college counselors have the opportunity to do some writing but not a whole lot.

As you complete each form, don't get discouraged if there are a few factors for which you're unable to assign a Career Score right away because of lack of information. Even if you've spent many hours gathering information about your career options, it's common to discover that you aren't aware of all the important details of a career. Try calling someone you know who might have the information you need or try locating some of the helpful materials presented back in Chapter 6. If you look hard enough, the information is bound to avail itself to you sooner or later.

Step 5.

This is the computational part of the exercise, in which you will determine a Total Career Value for each of the careers you've considered. This is done in two stages. First, go through each Career Analysis Form and multiply the Value Points for each factor by the Career Score you've assigned for that particular career. The resulting product becomes the Weighted Value for that factor. For example, on my Career Analysis form for college counselor, I assigned 30 Value Points to "Time with family" (as I did on all of my Career Analysis Forms) and a Career Score of 8 for that factor as it relates to College Counseling. Multiplying 30 by 8, I arrive at a score of 240. That number is placed in the fourth column (Weighted Value) of the Career Analysis Form.

After multiplying each line's value points by the career score for that factor, my Career Analysis Form for college counseling would look something like this:

Sample Career Analysis Form

Specific Career Option: College Counseling

Factors	Value Points		Career Score		Weighted Value
Time with family	30	×	8	=	240
Flexible work schedule	15	×	7	=	105
Stable income	10	×	9	=	90
Chance to help others	10	×	10	=	100
Opportunity for promotion	7	×	9	=	63
Social interaction	7	×	10	=	70
Opportunity to write	7	×	6	=	42
Health insurance	7	×	10	=	70
Professional atmosphere	7	×	9	=	63
			Total Career Points:		

Finally, add up all of the scores in the fourth column for each Career Option you've analyzed. When I do this for college counselor, my Total Career Score is 843.

Step 6.

The final step of the Career Analysis System is to determine which career option has the highest Total Career Points, as this career will become your tentative career choice. The career with the highest total score is the career option that best meets the career values that you've identified as most important to you. As such, it's likely to provide you with a high degree of job satisfaction, stability, and success. So that you can reach a sense of closure at this point in the career decision-making process, write in the career option that you've determined to be your tentative career choice at this time.

CONGRATULATIONS! You've made a career decision based on a thorough analysis of your interests, abilities, and values. You've analyzed the factors that matter to you most, and you've integrated all sorts of information into your decision. You've made a career decision that counts!

Career Analysis Form

Specific Career Option: _____

Factors	Value Points	Career Score	Weighted Value
_____	_____	_____	_____
_____	_____	_____	_____
_____	_____	_____	_____
_____	_____	_____	_____
_____	_____	_____	_____
_____	_____	_____	_____
_____	_____	_____	_____
_____	_____	_____	_____
_____	_____	_____	_____
_____	_____	_____	_____
_____	_____	_____	_____
_____	_____	_____	_____
_____	_____	_____	_____
_____	_____	_____	_____
_____	_____	_____	_____
_____	_____	_____	_____
_____	_____	_____	_____
_____	_____	_____	_____

Total Career Points: _____

9

Creating a Career Activities Timeline

If we use the analogy of building a new home to describe the process of career development, then making a tentative career choice is a lot like finishing the foundation. A tentative career choice represents the culmination of a great deal of time and energy that has been invested into the career decision-making process. But like completing the foundation work of a new home, this is certainly not the end of the process.

The purpose of this chapter is to assist you in the process of generating short-term goals and developing a detailed plan for carrying out your career decision. If there's one thing that counselors and psychologists have learned over the years, it's that setting short-term goals increases our chances of realizing long-term goals. In this chapter, you'll have the opportunity to think about educational and training requirements, financial needs, and other important factors that will undoubtedly influence how successful you'll be at achieving your career aspirations.

SETTING GOALS

Now that you've made a tentative decision of which career to pursue, it's time to make it happen! There are several things that you need to think about if you want to implement your tentative career choice successfully. The first thing you need to do is determine what steps are necessary for you to realize your goal.

The good news is that generating a list of steps probably won't require gathering much new information. If, in fact, you've already adequately researched the career that you've selected to pursue, then you should already know the answers to most of the important questions. Knowing how much educational preparation or training is required for entry into your career choice and what types of credentials or certifications are required, for example, are things that you probably learned in Chapter 6 when you completed the Career Information Job Shadow and Evaluation Forms associated with your tentative career choice.

In addition to your knowledge of specific job preparation requirements, there are several other important factors that will influence your career activities timeline. Making a career choice and carrying out that choice is probably not the *only* concern in your life right now—other aspects of your personal life certainly deserve your attention as well.

In Exercise 1.1 you thought about *all* of the things that you'd like to accomplish within the next 20 years or so. You may have listed goals that have little to do with career development and occupational achievement. As you think about implementing your career choice, consider other factors in your life and how they're going to affect your ability to carry out the remaining stages of the career decision-making process. The last thing that you want to do is focus too much on the career decision-making process at the expense of important interpersonal relationships and other responsibilities you have.

The bottom line is this: Career development—despite its importance—is only one part of who you are. Spiritual, mental, emotional, and physical well-being are also extremely important facets in your life, and each contributes to your overall life satisfaction. Make sure that you consider all relevant factors as you develop a timeline for carrying out your career goals.

Consider all relevant factors in your life as you develop a timeline for carrying out your career goals.

Consider how your career decisions will influence your family relationships. If you have significant others (e.g., children, a spouse), remember that your career decision will have a direct impact on their lives, and that they should play an important role in helping you clarify your goals and determining helpful strategies for accomplishing related tasks.

As with any goals-setting exercise, you need to try to develop a timeline that is realistic. Don't be too ambitious as you consider the length of time necessary to complete each of the steps required to realize your career goal. It's much better to set realistic goals, allowing yourself plenty of time to complete each task, rather than setting up a timeline that leaves no room for unexpected glitches.

consider Winnie

Winnie, a college student I met with a couple of years ago, had experienced frustration and anxiety because of her inability to accomplish certain goals in the timeline that she had created for herself. Winnie was a 38-year-old, single mother of four children, and was attending college with plans of becoming an accountant. She had decided that she should be able to achieve her goal within five years. She believed that it shouldn't take her any longer than that, and she needed the increase in salary potential as soon as possible.

Like many of today's college students, Winnie was working full-time. On an average day, she got up at about 5:00 in the morning to take care of housework and to study for an hour or so. Then, after getting her kids off to school, Winnie went to work, where she stayed until 4:00 each afternoon. After working all day she went back home to feed her kids, and, four nights a week she attended classes from 6:30 to 10:00.

It didn't take too long to understand why Winnie was experiencing a lot of frustration and anxiety. She was trying to accomplish something that may have been theoretically possible but that was placing great amounts of strain and stress on her personal life. Winnie and I worked on creating a more appropriate timeline that allowed her more flexibility and yet still kept her moving toward her career goal.

Balance in life is a very good thing.

The moral of Winnie's story, like so many others that I've seen over the years, is that balance in life is a very good thing. It's better to develop a career goals timeline that takes into account other aspects of your life rather than one that assumes that career decision making is all that matters.

The first thing you need to do to create your tentative career timeline is make a list of the major tasks necessary to enter the career you've selected. These tasks usually include such things as selecting a major, identifying financial resources available to you, completing course work, securing credentials or certifications, and/or obtaining a degree. If you've completed the exercises in Chapter 6, then you should have ready access to most of the information about educational and training requirements associated with your career choice.

EDUCATIONAL AND TRAINING OPPORTUNITIES

One of the most important factors in bringing your career goal to life involves obtaining the required education and training. There are a variety of educational and training opportunities available—some more appropriate than others, depending on the type of career you're pursuing. An overview of the various types of educational and training environments that are commonly utilized in career preparation might help you consider which avenue to pursue.

Vocational and Technical Schools

Vocational and technical schools are designed to provide students with job-specific training in specific fields of interest. Trade schools, technical institutes, and home-study or correspondence schools often fall into this category. Many people who are interested in gaining entry-level jobs in career fields as diverse as cosmetology, locksmithing, truck driving, and computer repair utilize vocational and technical school training in their career preparation.

The length of time required to complete vocational and technical school training can vary from a few months to a few years. Training usually involves practical classroom experience along with some traditional academics. Graduation from a vocational or technical school often results in a certificate of completion that can be used to obtain entry-level work in the field. Many employers also allow for some amount of on-the-job training upon hire.

Community and Junior Colleges

Some individuals attend community and junior colleges to take preparatory courses for obtaining a four-year degree. Most community and junior colleges offer a variety of courses that can be transferred as credit to most four-year institutions. Taking classes at community and junior colleges can be an excellent way to begin working on a four-year degree. Such courses usually cost less, include fewer students in the classroom, and are offered on a more flexible schedule than courses offered at a large four-year college or university.

Many other students attend two-year programs at community or junior colleges to gain the marketable skills preparatory to an entry-level career position. The types of two-year associate degree programs offered at most community or junior colleges are similar to the types of training offered at vocational and technical schools, but usually include additional options, such as programs in nursing, drafting, and emergency medical technology.

Still others attend community and junior colleges to engage in lifelong learning. Continuing education courses in a wide variety of career fields are usually offered at two-year colleges as an ongoing service to members of the community. Such courses might include computer software training, information on how to start your own business, or tips on completing your tax returns.

Four-Year Colleges and Universities

Four-year colleges and universities are attended by individuals whose career goals require at least a bachelor's degree. Students who attend such institutions will normally complete a general set of courses (usually referred to as general education or core curriculum requirements) in such subjects as history, English, and math, along with specialized courses directly associated with particular careers. Students "major" in one or two fields that serve as preparation for a career. They can also "minor" in related fields that can provide additional educational experiences related to a given career area.

Some careers require additional education beyond a bachelor's degree. Many professions, such as law, medicine, and psychology, require a master's or a doctorate degree for entry-level employment. The additional time required beyond a bachelor's degree to complete these types of programs varies from one or two years to six or seven.

Apprenticeship Programs

On-the-job training with limited classroom instruction is provided by most apprenticeship programs. Labor unions usually sponsor such programs although some are sponsored by actual employers or government agencies. A person who completes such an apprenticeship program (which can last anywhere from a few months to several years) is generally considered a "qualified" professional in that particular field.

Apprenticeship programs are popular methods of training in many careers associated with construction work, mechanical repair, and industrial production. Automobile mechanics, carpenters, heating and air conditioning specialists, and electricians are examples of professionals who often receive their training through apprenticeship programs.

The Armed Services

The armed forces can serve as an excellent training ground for individuals interested in a variety of different careers. Positions in the armed services include the same types of jobs that civilians work at, such as nursing, mechanics, and air traffic controlling. Many people join the army, air force, navy, marines, or coast guard as a way to gain valuable experience and master various job skills. Upon discharge from the armed services, many of these people then utilize the training they received to obtain civilian employment or as a springboard to other careers of interest.

Several different training programs and educational options are available to persons interested in the armed services. You've probably heard about ROTC (Reserve Officers' Training Corps) programs and the GI bill that can support the cost of an education at a college or university in return for service in a branch of the military. You might want to talk with a military recruiter if this option interests you.

If you have difficulty determining which type of educational or training situation is most appropriate for you, a career counselor or academic advisor may be able to point you in the right direction. Don't forget to utilize the information you gathered in Chapter 6, too. Sources such as the *Occupational Outlook Handbook* and the *Dictionary of Occupational Titles* can help you decide which type of training or educational opportunity to consider.

FACTORS TO CONSIDER WHEN SELECTING A SCHOOL OR TRAINING PROGRAM

Once you've determined what type of educational or training program is most appropriate for you, you'll need to select an appropriate institution. Making that decision requires you to consider a variety of factors, such as how well various institutions appear to meet your particular needs.

You should begin this process by identifying the institutions within your geographical limitations that offer the type of training you're in need of. If you're pursuing a career in automobile repair, for example, and you've decided to obtain an associate's degree in automotive technology from a community or junior college, then you'll want to determine which community and junior colleges you're able to attend. If you're pursuing a career that requires a bachelor's degree or additional academic credentials, then you'll want to take a look at the four-year colleges and universities that offer degree programs in your area of interest.

As you take a look at the various options available to you, consider how each institution measures up in terms of the following factors.

Tuition and Related Expenses

Obtaining adequate education and training required for entry into your career of interest can be quite a costly venture. Consider the cost of tuition as well as other costs associated with attending a particular institution, such as the cost of books, parking, transportation, supplies, and housing (if applicable).

Accreditation of the Institution

Most institutions are accredited in one way or another. Accreditation involves a group of professionals external to the institution making a determination regarding the quality of education or training offered at that particular site. A program that is accredited is one that has been "approved" by external reviewers.

Academic Calendar

Most colleges and universities conduct classes on either a quarter or semester system. Institutions that operate on the quarter system usually have four 10- or 12-week terms during the course of the year. Those that operate on the semester system usually offer classes in two 15- or 16-week terms as well as during selected summer sessions. Technical and vocational schools vary in their schedules but usually offer a variety of different programs.

Requirements for Admission

Review the requirements for admission to an institution to make sure that you can meet them. Grade-point averages from previous educational experiences (e.g., high school grades) and scores on standardized tests (e.g., the SAT or ACT) are usually considered along with letters of recommendation and a personal essay.

Length of Program

Training programs, especially those offered by an apprenticeship program or a technical or vocational training center, can vary dramatically in length. Considering other responsibilities in your life, the length of time involved in securing the credentials or certificates necessary for you to pursue your career can be an important factor in your decision of where to obtain your training.

Financial Aid/Grants/Scholarships

Consider financial resources available to you for carrying out your career plan. These days, even one year of education can be extremely costly. Determining methods for funding your education or training is an important aspect of career planning that is often forgotten. It's best to have an established plan for funding your career goals so that you don't find yourself without the resources to complete your training. Consider current funding sources as well as alternative sources that may be available to you in the future. Financial aid counselors at most colleges and universities can provide you with helpful information. They'll be able to project costs associated with attending college, and they'll inform you of local and national scholarships and grants for which you might qualify.

SELECTING A MAJOR

Once you've determined where you're going to obtain your educational training and experience, you may have to (depending on your career goal) select an appropriate major. Consulting a career counselor at the institution and talking with an advisor are two of the best ways to determine which major is appropriate for you given your particular career interests.

An advisor will be able to tell you the exact courses you'll need for completing a particular degree program as well as help you structure a timeline for accomplishing those tasks. If you've decided to seek a career as a chemist or a biologist, then the appropriate major is fairly obvious. But many careers, contrary to popular belief, don't necessarily require one particular academic course of study. Many law schools, for example, encourage prospective applicants to major in any one of a variety of disciplines, ranging from English and journalism to political science and history. Medical schools accept applicants with a wide range of backgrounds and experience, including students with degrees in psychology, math, and biology—just to name a few.

The important thing is to meet with the persons who are likely to provide you with helpful advice. Career counselors, advisors, and people you know who are currently employed in the career you're pursuing are often very reliable sources of information.

CREATING A CAREER ACTIVITIES TIMELINE

As you continue to make decisions about education and training related to your career choice, develop a timeline for completing the various steps involved in realizing your career goal. Think about the barriers you identified in Chapter 7 and make sure to allow ample time in your career plan for addressing them. It's all part of careful, realistic planning for your career.

So, if you haven't recently done so, refer to Chapter 7 to review the work you completed relevant to the perception of career-related barriers. After reviewing that material, you'll be ready to complete Exercise 9.1, Career Preparation Requirements, and Exercise 9.2, Creating the Timeline.

9.1 CAREER PREPARATION REQUIREMENTS

This exercise helps you organize the information you've gathered so that you'll be better able to construct a career timeline. An example is provided to illustrate how this is to be done.

Begin by noting the different requirements associated with your tentative career choice.

Sample Career Preparation Requirements

Tentative Career Choice: _____ Corporate Lawyer _____

List below the educational and training requirements associated with your career choice:

Educational Requirements

Completion of a bachelor's degree; admission to law school;

completion of law school course work

Training Requirements

Internship with practicing lawyer

Licensure/Certification/Credentials Requirements

Pass the bar exam

Additional Requirements

Work on developing my public speaking skills

Considering the other responsibilities in your life (in other words, making sure that you leave enough time to ensure that your personal needs are taken care of), how long do you think it'll take you to complete the educational and training requirements listed above?   Eight years

Your Career Preparation Requirements

Tentative Career Choice: _____

List below the educational and training requirements associated with your career choice:

Educational Requirements

_____

_____

_____

Training Requirements

_____

Licensure/Certification/Credentials Requirements

_____

Additional Requirements

_____

Considering the other responsibilities in your life (in other words, making sure that you leave enough time to ensure that your personal needs are taken care of), how long do you think it'll take you to complete the educational and training requirements listed above? _____

There will be many steps along the way that'll help you complete the requirements you've identified.

For example, a student I recently worked with, Chi, decided to become a lawyer. In addition to completing a bachelor's degree and going to law school, Chi will have to pass the bar exam in the state in which she decides to practice law. The steps toward accomplishing these tasks include determining an appropriate major, applying for admission to law school, and so forth. As she considers the many steps along the way, keeping in mind ways to accomplish each step and the time that will be involved, Chi might draft some plans such as these:

STEP: Select an Appropriate Major

Plan of Action to Accomplish This Step

Meet with my academic advisor and talk with my father's lawyer for some advice

Other Things I Need to Consider When Completing This Step

My academic advisor is only available on Friday afternoons, and I work on Fridays.

I'll have to get a day off in a couple of weeks or find out if I can make an individual

appointment.

Approximate Time for Completing This Step

By the end of next week

STEP: Applying for Law School

Plan of Action to Accomplish This Step

Take the Law School Admissions Test (LSAT) Preparation course; Meet with

the pre-law advisor to get application forms; Take the LSAT

Other Things I Need to Consider When Completing This Step

The law school advisor is available for drop-in appointments every morning until

11:00. I'll need to go by on Tuesday or Thursday to get the LSAT application forms.

Approximate Time for Completing This Step

March or April of my senior year

Based on the information you've been able to gather relevant to your career choice, list below the various steps you'll need to take to accomplish the educational and training requirements you've already identified. (Make additional copies of this form if necessary.)

STEP: _____

Plan of Action to Accomplish This Step

_____

_____

_____

Other Things I Need to Consider When Completing This Step

_____

_____

_____

Approximate Time for Completing This Step

_____

STEP: _____

Plan of Action to Accomplish This Step

_____

_____

_____

Other Things I Need to Consider When Completing This Step

_____

_____

_____

Approximate Time for Completing This Step

_____

STEP: _____

Plan of Action to Accomplish This Step

_____

_____

_____

Other Things I Need to Consider When Completing This Step

_____

_____

_____

Approximate Time for Completing This Step

_____

9.2 CREATING THE TIMELINE

Before developing a timeline for reaching your career goal, review some of the topics we've discussed in this chapter regarding goal setting outlined in the box that follows.

Factors to Consider When Creating Your Career Activities Timeline

Be Realistic	It makes no sense to create an overly ambitious timeline. Doing so only sets up a situation that tends to foster frustration and anxiety.
Create a Balance	Don't forget the many responsibilities and other important needs in your life. You'll need to address these areas of your life as you continue to pursue your career. Be sure to leave ample time to devote to these personal issues as you work toward realizing your career goals.
Ask Others to Share Their Perspectives	The social support network you've established can be a great source of advice and support throughout the career decision-making process. As you consider a timeline for accomplishing the many tasks associated with your career choice, these individuals can be especially helpful to you. Bounce your plans off of some of them, and see how they react to your ideas.
Remember That This Timeline Is Tentative	No matter how organized we are, sometimes there are circumstances that alter our plans. Allow yourself the flexibility to alter some of your plans and goal dates in the future if the need should arise.

Your Tentative Career Timeline

As you review the work you completed in Exercise 9.1, you should be able to place the specific tasks you need to accomplish into one of the time frames shown below.

Today's Date _____

Career-Related Tasks to Accomplish Within the Next Month

TASK   COMPLETION GOAL DATE

_____   _____

_____   _____

_____   _____

_____   _____

_____   _____

Career-Related Tasks to Accomplish Within the Next Two to Three Months

TASK   COMPLETION GOAL DATE

_____   _____

_____   _____

_____   _____

_____   _____

_____   _____

Career-Related Tasks to Accomplish Within the Next Three to Six Months

TASK   COMPLETION GOAL DATE

_____   _____

_____   _____

_____   _____

_____   _____

_____   _____

Career-Related Tasks to Accomplish Within the Next Six Months to a Year

TASK   COMPLETION GOAL DATE

_____   _____

_____   _____

_____   _____

_____   _____

_____   _____

Career-Related Tasks to Accomplish Within the Next Two to Three Years

TASK   COMPLETION GOAL DATE

_____   _____

_____   _____

_____   _____

_____   _____

_____   _____

Career-Related Tasks to Accomplish Within the Next Three to Five Years

TASK   COMPLETION GOAL DATE

_____   _____

_____   _____

_____   _____

_____   _____

_____   _____

Career-Related Tasks to Accomplish Within the Next Five to Ten Years

TASK   COMPLETION GOAL DATE

_____   _____

_____   _____

_____   _____

_____   _____

_____   _____

Because goal-setting is such an important part of career decision making, make sure that you periodically review your list of goals and the tentative timeline you've developed. As you review your progress on a regular basis, you'll be able to refine your goals as necessary and develop new strategies for accomplishing the important tasks you've identified.

10

Looking and Planning Ahead

As you firm up your tentative career choice and complete the steps that'll allow you to fully realize your career goals, you'll find yourself completing the exploration stage of career development and beginning the establishment stage. Although the focus of this book is on the exploration stage of the career decision-making process, the purpose of this concluding chapter is to provide an overview of the activities involved in the establishment, maintenance, and disengagement phases of career development and to discuss ways that you might modify the career exploration process to fit your own individual needs.

ESTABLISHMENT AND MAINTENANCE STAGES OF CAREER DEVELOPMENT

One of the first things you'll do as you become established within a career is learn about the intricacies of that career. I've been working as a career counselor for many years, but that certainly doesn't mean that I've learned everything there is to know about being a career counselor. I'm constantly learning new things and understanding concepts in greater depth.

During the establishment and maintenance stages of career development, you'll discover ways to increase job satisfaction and happiness. It may mean preparing for promotions and job advancement or making a minor career change, such as looking for a supervisory position in the same career field or trying to update and retool in order to remain marketable in your chosen career.

Many working adults seek career counseling because they would like to find ways to increase their job satisfaction or their ability to be successful at work. Evaluating current job satisfaction can often be a helpful first step in that process. A brief job satisfaction questionnaire is provided in Appendix E for your use in the future. Talking with coworkers and supervisors is also a good way to get some assistance in this area.

Linda, a lawyer I worked with a few years ago, had been working in the banking industry for almost 20 years. She was generally satisfied with her career, but she wanted to find out if there were ways that she could use her talents and skills to begin some type of an entrepreneurial activity. Linda knew that one day she would like to own a small business, and she was beginning to think that the time was right.

Consider Linda

Linda was in the maintenance stage of career development, but she wanted to create some new challenges to keep her level of work motivation high and maintain a high level of career satisfaction and success.

There's always some way to improve our work situation and career satisfaction.

Throughout the establishment and maintenance stages within a career, it's important to evaluate your work situation periodically. There's almost always something that can be done to improve our work situation and, in turn, our career satisfaction. Seeking ways to improve your work situation should be an ongoing process as should your commitment to making career development a lifelong process.

THE DISENGAGEMENT STAGE OF CAREER DEVELOPMENT

According to Dr. Super, the fifth and final stage of career development is *disengagement*. It's during disengagement that we begin to prepare for a complete change in career focus. For some, disengagement from a career may mean making a major career change, such as moving from a career as an electrical engineer to a career as a math teacher. For many of us, disengagement will very simply mean retirement. Though the focus of this book is on the exploration stage of career decision making, there are a few things about disengagement that it might be helpful for you to know.

Probably the most important piece of advice regarding disengagement is, very simply put, PREPARE!

The time to prepare for retirement *is* now. It's *never* too early to begin thinking about financial security, emotional stability, physical well being, and leisure interests. The time to figure out what types of financial plans are available for retirement is now. The time to develop hobbies and leisure interests is now. The time to take care of physical needs by eating healthy and staying in shape is now. Whether you're wrapping up the exploration stage of career decision making, establishing yourself within a selected career, entering the maintenance stage, or getting ready to retire, preparation is the key.

REFINING THE CAREER DECISION-MAKING PROCESS TO MEET YOUR NEEDS

Dr. Super's model of career development has been useful for hundreds of thousands of students who have engaged in the career decision-making process, but that does not mean that it'll work without fail for everyone. For some, additional exploration activities are necessary before they are comfortable making a career choice. For others, it may simply take more time than average to complete all of the activities associated with the career decision-making process. You may need to adapt Dr. Super's model of career development to fit your particular life circumstances.

As time goes on, remember the steps in the career decision-making process that have worked well for you.

As you reflect on the career decision-making process, think about which steps have worked particularly well for you. Perhaps the self-assessments of interests and skills in Chapter 3 played an important role in your career decisions. Or maybe the increased self-awareness provided by an exploration of values in Chapter 4 helped you reach a tentative decision you're pleased with. Then again, you may have found the list of sources for collecting information about occupations in Chapter 6 one of the most helpful aspects of the process. If you're able to determine which parts of the book work especially well for you, then you'll know what activities and exercises to complete again in the future.

As mentioned before, most everyone recycles through the career decision-making process at least a couple of times throughout their lives. If you're aware of which exercises are particularly helpful to you, then you'll know which parts of the book to work through again in the future when a career change is appropriate.

Reynaldo was 42 years old and had worked for a large aluminum recycling factory since graduating from college with a degree in engineering at age 24. He had been successful in his job and had received a series of promotions over the years. Eventually Reynaldo was promoted to the position of Assistant Director of Research and Development. All seemed to be going well for Reynaldo until he was laid off along with many other mid-level managers. After 18 years of steady work, Reynaldo found himself unemployed.

When Reynaldo and I met, one of the first things I recognized about him was that he was very satisfied working in the aluminum industry. He recounted several instances in the past in which he had received job offers to work somewhere else but declined those opportunities because he enjoyed his work so much. Now unemployed, Reynaldo explained to me that he wanted to find a new job that would be as similar to the one he had become accustomed to as possible.

There was certainly no need for Reynaldo to evaluate his interests and abilities or reflect on his values. Most of the exercises in Chapters 3 and 4, although essential for most people, would not have been the proper place of focus for Reynaldo. He was keenly aware of the important aspects of his self-concept. The focus of our work together, then, was targeted more on the latter stages of the exploration process.

Because it had been so long since Reynaldo had applied for a job, we spent some time working on a résumé and discussing important tips when completing job applications. We engaged in some practice interviews and discussed methods for locating job openings in research and development for individuals with a background in engineering and aluminum recycling. In other words, we focused in on those activities that were likely to benefit Reynaldo most directly.

Because of the time we spent on these tasks, Reynaldo was able to obtain a satisfying new position as the Director of Training and Development with a large recycling company in a neighboring town.

Consider Reynaldo

Each of us has unique characteristics that influence our career decisions. When the time comes for you to recycle through the career decision-making process, you'll need to recognize which stages apply to your particular situation. Recycling may not require completion of each and every activity in this book. Instead, there may be a few chapters and exercises in particular that apply to your life situation, and it'll be up to you to determine which parts of the book will be most beneficial to you at any given point. Rereading Chapter 2 and completing Exercise 2.1 again will always be a good starting point. It's one helpful way to figure out, at *any* point in time, which sections of the book apply most directly to your situation.

Our unique characteristics influence our career decisions.

CONCLUSION

My primary hope in writing this book has been to impart to you the important things to consider when making career decisions and to show you how to engage in career decision making effectively. That way, as you recycle through the career decision-making process in the future, you'll know how to go about making career decisions that count.

In particular, I hope you've learned

- That making career decisions requires a comprehensive understanding of who you are, what Dr. Super referred to as your self-concept.

- How critical it is that you have a good understanding of your personality, interests, abilities, and values.
- How to integrate all aspects of your self-concept when making career decisions, thus maximizing your chances of career satisfaction and success.
- Valuable ways of thinking about potential barriers to your career choice.
- Methods for overcoming potential barriers.

Most of all, I hope you've realized that investing time and energy into the career decision-making process is well worth it.

Throughout this book you have gained tools that will assist you making career decisions. Utilize those tools, invest yourself into the process, and you'll be sure to reap the benefits. Our careers are an integral part of who we are. Make sure that you do all that you can to maximize your chances of occupational satisfaction and success. If you do, you'll continue to make career decisions that count!

Occupations Considered Most Attractive by Persons with Certain Psychological Types

ENFJ

Religiously Oriented
  Occupations
Home Economist
Optometrist

Musician or Composer
Counselor
Artist or Entertainer
Dental Hygienist

Physician: Family,
  General Practice
Designer
Child Care Worker

ENFP

Counselor or
  Psychologist
Teacher: Arts, Health,
  Special Education
Researcher

Religiously Oriented
  Occupations
Writer or Editor
Musician or Composer
Social Scientist

Computer Professional
Public Relations Worker
Administrator: Education

ENTJ

Consultant: Management
Human Resources
Computer Professional
Physician: Family

Manager: Sales
Manager: Executive
Credit Investigator or
  Mortgage Broker

Marketing Professional
Administrator: Education
Administrator: Health

ENTP

Photographer
Marketing Professional
Writer or Journalist
Computer Professional

Credit Investigator or
  Mortgage Broker
Psychiatrist
Engineer

Construction Worker
Artist or Entertainer
Research Worker

ESFJ

Teacher
Administrator: Student Personnel
Manager: Office

Religiously Oriented Occupations
Dental Assistant
Child Care Worker
Home Economist

Hair Dresser or Cosmetologist
Receptionist
Food Service Worker

ESFP

Child Care Worker
Teacher
Designer
Receptionist

Transportation Worker
Factory Supervisor
Library Worker
Cashier

Lifeguard or Recreation Attendant
Food Service Worker

ESTJ

Manager: Small Business, Factory, Sales
Purchasing Agent
Teacher: Trade or Technical

Law Enforcement Worker
Factory Supervisor
Public Service or Community Health Worker

Cleaning Service Worker
School Bus Driver
Insurance Agent or Broker
Social Services Worker

ESTP

Marketing Professional
Law Enforcement Worker
Carpenter

Manager: Small Business or Government
Auditor
Craft Worker

Farmer
Laborer
Transportation Worker
Factory Worker

INFJ

Religiously Oriented Occupations
Counselor, Psychologist, or Social Worker

Psychiatrist
Teacher
Consultant: Education
Doctor or Nurse

Architect
Fine Artist
Research Assistant
Marketing Professional

INFP

Artist or Entertainer
Psychiatrist
Counselor, Psychologist, or Social Worker

Architect
Research Assistant
Social Scientist
Writer or Editor

Laboratory Technologist
Consultant: Education
Therapist: Physical

INTJ

Architect
Computer Professional
Consultant: Management
Manager: Executive

Human Resources Personnel
Lawyer or Judge
Research Worker

Social Services Worker
Engineer
Scientist: Life or Physical

INTP

Computer Professional	Food Service Worker	Social Scientist
Architect	Surveyor	Writer or Editor
Research Assistant	Manager: Executive	Photographer
Fine Artist		

ISFJ

Nursing	Administrator: Social Services	Health Service Worker
Teacher	Librarian	School Bus Driver
Religiously Oriented Occupations	Physician: Family, General Practice	Food Service
		Private Household Worker

ISFP

Nurse	Carpenter	Bookkeeper
Storekeeper	Surveyor	Cleaning Service Worker
Law Enforcement Worker	Clerical Supervisor	Cook
	Dental Assistant	

ISTJ

Manager: Small Business, Factory	Law Enforcement Worker	Purchasing Agent
Accountant	School Principal	Computer Professional
Manager: Executive	School Bus Driver	Dentist
		Steelworker

ISTP

Farmer	Law Enforcement Worker	Transportation Worker
Military Officer or Enlistee	Engineering or Science Technician	Dental Assistant
Engineer	Coal Miner	Laborer
		Mechanic

Scoring Instructions for Chapter 3 Exercises

EXERCISE 3.1: WHAT'S MY TYPE? (Pages 28–30) AND
EXERCISE 3.2: CAREER DREAMING (Page 31)

To score Exercises 3.1 and 3.2, you'll need to determine which "work environment" best describes each of the careers included on your list. "Work environment" refers to Dr. Roe's categories for describing career types: Service, Business Contact, Organization, Technology, Outdoors, Science, General Culture, and Arts and Entertainment. Refer to Table B.1 on the following page for Dr. Roe's classification system.

Next to each of the careers included in your lists found on pages 30 and 31, write the work environment type that *best* describes that particular career. If you're unable to determine which work environment is most appropriate for a particular career, you might ask a career counselor or teacher for some advice or consult Appendix C for a list of careers arranged by occupational type.

An example might help to clarify this scoring procedure. One of the careers I would probably include on my Dream List would be "actor." Because being an actor involves artistic talent and creativity, and because the description of the Arts and Entertainment work environment is the best description of the types of things an actor is involved in, I would write the words ARTS AND ENTERTAINMENT next to "actor." Another career I would include on my Dream List would be pediatrician. If I looked at Table B.1 and was not sure which work environment is associated with being a pediatrician, then I could turn to Appendix C. Referring to Appendix C, I'd discover that the appropriate occupational type for pediatrician is Science.

table b.1	Summary of work environments.

WORK ENVIRONMENT	SAMPLE OCCUPATIONS	CHARACTERISTICS OF PEOPLE WHO LIKE WORKING IN THESE ENVIRONMENTS
Service	Social worker Marriage counselor Police officer Occupational therapist	Enjoy serving and attending to the personal tastes, needs, and welfare of other people; obtain a strong sense of satisfaction from helping and/or protecting other people.
Business Contact	Real estate agent Salesperson Insurance agent Public relations specialist	Enjoy persuading other people to engage in a particular course of action, such as the purchase of a commodity or service.
Organization	Employment manager Accountant Business executive Small-business owner	Enjoy engaging in tasks that involve a high level of organization and precision; often satisfied by supervising or managing others.
Technology	Electrical engineer Mechanic Truck driver Carpenter	Enjoy producing, transporting, and/or fixing things; more satisfied working with tools and objects than with people.
Outdoors	Gardener Wildlife specialist Farmer Horticulturalist	Enjoy working in outdoor settings; often favor working with animals and plants rather than with people.
Science	Chiropractor X-ray technician Dentist Paleontologist	Enjoy working with scientific theory and its application to real-world problems.
General Culture	Lawyer High school teacher Librarian Historian	Enjoy interacting with groups of people in an effort to preserve and/or transmit knowledge and cultural heritage.
Arts and Entertainment	Interior decorator Professional athlete Choreographer Art teacher	Enjoy environments that provide opportunities for artistic expression and/or the use of special skills in an entertainment industry.

Go ahead now and write on pages 30 and 31 the primary occupational type (Service, Business Contact, Organization, Technology, Outdoors, Science, General Culture, and Arts and Entertainment) next to each of the careers included in your lists generated in Exercises 3.1 and 3.2.

Next, fill in the "scores" for each work environment category by awarding 5 points for each occurrence of the occupational types included in your lists. For example, if my list of careers generated from Exercise 3.1 included one Arts and Entertainment career, four Service careers, and three Science careers, then I would award 5 points to Arts and Entertainment (because my list included one Arts and Entertainment career), 20 points to Service, and 15 points to Science. My scores for this exercise would look like this:

Scores from Exercise 3.1

Service	Business Contact	Organization	Technology	Outdoors	Science	General Culture	Arts and Entertainment
20	0	0	0	0	15	0	5

Repeat this process for assigning scores to each of the career types for Exercise 3.2

EXERCISE 3.3: ACTIVITIES RATINGS (Pages 32–33)

This exercise also results in a score for each of the work environments. The total score for each type is determined by adding together the ratings you assigned to each of the activities representing a particular occupational type. Your Service score, for example, is the sum of your ratings for the five Service types of activities included in Exercise 3.3.

The guide shown below indicates which items in Exercise 3.3 represent each work environment. For example, item numbers 5, 8, 26, 32, and 39 represent service careers. Above each item number, fill in the ratings you gave the item in Exercise 3.3. Then simply add up your scores in each occupational category to determine your total scores. Each total score should be somewhere between 5 and 25 points. Place the score for each career type in the appropriate spaces in Exercise 5.1 (p. 50).

Service:

_____ + _____ + _____ + _____ + _____ = _____
  5   8   26   32   39

Business Contact:

_____ + _____ + _____ + _____ + _____ = _____
  2   12   24   33   36

Organization:

_____ + _____ + _____ + _____ + _____ = _____
  3   11   14   18   22

Technology:

_____ + _____ + _____ + _____ + _____ = _____
  15   21   27   35   40

Outdoors:

_____ + _____ + _____ + _____ + _____ = _____
  6   10   16   30   38

Science:

_____ + _____ + _____ + _____ + _____ = _____
  1   7   17   20   25

General Culture:

_____ + _____ + _____ + _____ + _____ = _____
  4   13   19   29   37

Arts & Entertainment:

_____ + _____ + _____ + _____ + _____ = _____
  9   23   28   31   34

EXERCISE 3.4: LINKING THE PAST TO THE PRESENT
(Pages 34–35)

To score this exercise, follow the same procedure used for scoring Exercise 3.3. The guide shown below indicates which items in Exercise 3.4 represent each occupational type. As you did for Exercise 3.3, add up the ratings for each type and record them in the appropriate spaces in Exercise 5.1.

Service:

_____ + _____ + _____ + _____ + _____ = _____
　2　　　　10　　　　　17　　　　　25　　　　　36

Business Contact:

_____ + _____ + _____ + _____ + _____ = _____
　3　　　　13　　　　　23　　　　　28　　　　　37

Organization:

_____ + _____ + _____ + _____ + _____ = _____
　7　　　　20　　　　　24　　　　　29　　　　　35

Technology:

_____ + _____ + _____ + _____ + _____ = _____
　6　　　　21　　　　　26　　　　　34　　　　　38

Outdoors:

_____ + _____ + _____ + _____ + _____ = _____
　4　　　　12　　　　　15　　　　　30　　　　　39

Science:

_____ + _____ + _____ + _____ + _____ = _____
　5　　　　11　　　　　18　　　　　22　　　　　32

General Culture:

_____ + _____ + _____ + _____ + _____ = _____
　8　　　　16　　　　　27　　　　　31　　　　　40

Arts & Entertainment:

_____ + _____ + _____ + _____ + _____ = _____
　1　　　　9　　　　　14　　　　　19　　　　　33

EXERCISE 3.5: HOW WELL DO YOU DO WHAT YOU DO?
(Pages 36–37)

As you did for Exercises 3.3 and 3.4, you simply need to determine the total rating points for the skills representing each occupational type. The guide shown below indicates which skill items in Exercise 3.5 represent each occupational type. Total scores for each type should be recorded in the appropriate spaces in Exercise 5.1.

Service:

_____ + _____ + _____ + _____ + _____ = _____
　1　　　　13　　　　　17　　　　　23　　　　　30

Business Contact:

_____ + _____ + _____ + _____ + _____ = _____
　5　　　　15　　　　　25　　　　　35　　　　　39

Organization:

_____ + _____ + _____ + _____ + _____ = _____
　4　　　　9　　　　　16　　　　　20　　　　　29

Technology:

_____ + _____ + _____ + _____ + _____ = _____
　10　　　　18　　　　　26　　　　　33　　　　　37

Outdoors:

_____ + _____ + _____ + _____ + _____ = _____
　2　　　　8　　　　　24　　　　　31　　　　　38

Science:

_____ + _____ + _____ + _____ + _____ = _____
　12　　　　21　　　　　27　　　　　32　　　　　36

General Culture:

_____ + _____ + _____ + _____ + _____ = _____
　3　　　　7　　　　　19　　　　　22　　　　　28

Arts & Entertainment:

_____ + _____ + _____ + _____ + _____ = _____
　6　　　　11　　　　　14　　　　　34　　　　　40

Sample Occupations Arranged by Type of Work Environment

SERVICE

Barber
Bartender
Career counselor
Chef
Child care worker
Clinical psychologist
Correctional officer
Counseling psychologist
Counselor (general)
Day care worker
Dental assistant
Detective
Dietician/nutritionist

Emergency medical technician
FBI agent
Firefighter
Flight attendant
Food service worker
Hairdresser
Highway patrol officer
Homemaker
Hospital attendant
Lifeguard
Occupational therapist
Physical therapist

Police officer
Police sergeant
Practical nurse
Prison guard
Probation officer
Psychotherapist
Religious worker
Server (restaurant)
Sheriff
Social worker
Taxi driver
Teacher's aide
YMCA/YWCA director

BUSINESS CONTACT

Auctioneer
Automobile salesperson
Insurance salesperson
Insurance agent/broker

Mortgage broker
Promoter
Public relations specialist
Real estate agent

Retail/wholesale dealer
Sales representative
Traveling salesperson

ORGANIZATION

Accountant
Actuary
Administrative assistant
Armed services officer
Auditor
Banker
Bank teller
Bookkeeper
Business executive
Business manager
Buyer
Cashier
Certified public
  accountant
Chief executive officer
Clerical supervisor
Court reporter
Department store clerk

Employment manager
Financial manager
Financial planner
General office clerk
Government executive
Health administrator
Hotel clerk
Hotel manager
Human resources director
Management consultant
Medical records
  technician
Office clerk
Office manager
Payroll clerk
Personnel manager
Politician
Postal worker

Public official
Purchasing agent
Receptionist
Restaurant manager
Retail sales manager
Sales clerk
Sales manager
Secretary
Shipping and receiving
  clerk
Small business owner
Statistician
Stenographer
Stockbroker
Typist
Warehouse supervisor
Word processing
  specialist

TECHNOLOGY

Aerospace engineer
Aircraft mechanic
Applied scientist
Autobody repairer
Automobile mechanic
Aviator/pilot
Bricklayer
Building contractor
Bus driver
Butcher
Carpenter
Chemical engineer
Civil engineer
Computer repairperson
Construction worker

Draftsperson
Electrician
Electronics equipment
  repairperson
Engineer (general)
Engineering technician
Engine mechanic
Factory worker
Farm equipment
  mechanic
General repairperson
Heating, air conditioning,
  and refrigeration
  technician
Heavy equipment
  specialist

Jeweler
Machinist
Mechanic
Mechanical engineer
Painter
Pipefitter
Plumber
Printer
Printing press operator
Sheet metal worker
Steel worker
Tailor
Truck driver
Welder

OUTDOOR

Agricultural specialist
Agronomist
Botanist
Dairy hand
Farmer
Floriculturalist

Forest ranger
Game warden
Gardener
Horticulturalist
Landscape architect
Rancher

Surveyor
Teamster
Tractor driver
Tree surgeon
Wildlife specialist

SCIENCE

Anthropologist
Archaeologist
Astronomer
Audiologist
Biochemist
Biologist
Cardiologist
Chemist
Chiropractor
Dentist
Experimental psychologist
Laboratory technician
Life scientist
Mathematician
Medical specialist
Medical technician
Meteorologist
Neurologist
Nurse
Obstetrician
Oceanographer
Ophthalmologist
Optometrist
Paleontologist
Pathologist
Pediatrician
Pharmacist
Physician
Physicist
Podiatrist
Psychiatrist
Psychologist
Radiologist
Research scientist
Science teacher
Sociologist
Speech pathologist
Surgeon
University/college
    professor (science field)
Veterinarian
X-ray technician

GENERAL CULTURE

Broadcaster
Clergy (minister, rabbi,
    priest)
Editor
Educational administrator
Elementary school
    teacher
High school teacher
Historian
Interpreter
Journalist
Judge
Law clerk
Lawyer
Librarian
Newscaster
News commentator
Paralegal assistant
Philosopher
Preschool teacher
Radio announcer
Reporter
School principal
School superintendent
Social scientist
University/college
    professor
Urban planner

ARTS AND ENTERTAINMENT

Actor
Advertising artist
Advertising writer
Architect
Art teacher
Art critic
Artist
Athletic coach
Author/writer
Choreographer
Cinematographer
Commercial artist
Composer
Cosmetologist
Dance instructor
Dancer
Designer
Drama teacher
Entertainer
Fine artist
Graphic designer
Interior decorator
Music arranger
Musician
Performing artist
Photographer
Professional athlete
Race car driver
Screenwriter
Sculptor
Singer
Stage designer

Job Search Strategies

Probably the most important thing to remember about job search strategies is that the more sources you're willing to utilize, the better your chances are for locating the type of job that you really want. By expanding your job search strategies to include multiple sources, you increase your chances of finding out about a significantly greater number of jobs. The following list provides you with the many helpful sources that are available to you so that you can exhaust all possibilities seeking part-time, volunteer, or full-time employment.

CLASSIFIED ADVERTISEMENTS

Many people find out about job openings by reading the classified ads in their local newspapers. In large towns, there are often hundreds of jobs in a variety of fields listed in each week's Sunday paper. These job opportunities are arranged alphabetically by job type and can provide you with a quick reference to job openings in your area. Even in smaller towns, many job openings are listed in the classified ads. If you're hoping to work somewhere other than where you're currently living, then you should check the classified ads of the newspaper published in that particular city. Remember that classified job listings, however, represent a very small percentage of existing job openings. That's why you'll want to use a variety of other sources when searching for a job.

YOUR NETWORK OF CONNECTIONS

These days, with increased competition for jobs, many people are realizing that their personal and professional connections often play an important role in securing a job. The more people you know who are willing to help you locate the type of job you're seeking, the better off you'll be. The time to begin making these connections is now—well before you're ready to begin working full-time in your selected career field. Your network of connections can include personal friends, family members, community and religious leaders, and other persons who can help you locate potential openings in your field.

TEACHERS AND COUNSELORS

High school and college teachers who are actively involved in their communities are often valuable sources for locating job openings related to your selected career. You might try asking some of your teachers for information they have about job openings. At the very least, they may be able to point you in certain directions that'll increase your chances of finding a good job. Career counselors can also be a helpful source of information about employment opportunities. In addition to offering the same type of help teachers often provide, career counselors often receive actual job announcements and can help you identify positions that are available in your area of interest.

JOB POSTINGS

Many jobs that are available in a community are included in job postings, lists of jobs that are available within a company or an organization. Most college and university career planning and placement centers post jobs in cabinets or on bulletin boards so that you can quickly see what opportunities are available both on and off campus. Many large companies also list current openings in weekly or bi-weekly job bulletins. These types of bulletins usually consist of a printout of current jobs for which the company is accepting applications. You might want to make a quick phone call to the human resources directors of organizations that interest you and ask for the latest copy of their job bulletin.

TELEPHONE JOB LISTINGS

To cut down on the costs associated with advertising job openings, many companies—including most state and local governments—have developed telephone "hot lines." These hot lines usually list all openings at a company or organization, informing prospective applicants of important information such as salary range and educational requirements. These job hot lines are sometimes listed in the yellow pages of telephone directories. You can find out if a certain company operates a job hot line by calling the human resources department of that company.

COLLEGE AND UNIVERSITY CAREER CENTERS

Check with your college's career center to find out what services are available to help you locate potential jobs related to your career choice. Full-service career centers almost always have placement services that include job postings—not only for jobs in the local community but for jobs across the country as well. This is especially true for full-time opportunities in professional fields such as teaching and law. In fact, many schools of education, law, and business (especially at large universities) have their own career services that can help students learn about job openings in their respective fields.

CAREER FAIRS

Career fairs are large organized gatherings of many employers looking for new employees to join their companies. These fairs are usually organized by high schools, colleges, and universities or by large civic and community groups. Job fairs are a good way to find out what companies are hiring in your area and what opportunities exist within other regions of the country. If you decide to attend a career fair, make sure that you dress appropriately and take copies of your résumé along: You never know when someone you meet at a career fair might become a prospective employer.

COMPUTER NETWORK JOB LISTINGS

With the advent of the Internet and other computer network systems, it has become possible for you to find out about national and even international job opportunities related to your career choice in a matter of seconds. If you have access to the Internet, utilize the system to assist you in your job search. There are many "gopher sites" that actually list job openings and a few "world wide web sites" and "home pages" that might even allow you to post your resume electronically so that prospective employers can review your credentials. A computer network specialist or a career counselor might be able to teach you how to "surf" the Internet as a potential job search strategy.

ONE-STOP CAREER CENTERS

Because of the focus on school-to-work transitions in recent years, the federal government has sponsored the development of "one-stop career centers." Operated by state and local governments, one-stop career centers are designed to help members of the community with all stages involved in the career decision-making process. The focus of such centers, however, is usually to assist individuals who are looking for jobs in the area. Although there are only a few regions of the country that have developed one-stop career centers, check to see if there is such a center in your community.

EMPLOYMENT AGENCIES

Although at one time employment agencies and "headhunters" were one of the most commonly utilized sources for finding out what jobs were available, these organizations are less commonly utilized nowadays. Nevertheless, you might want to find out if an employment agency can help you locate job openings related to your career choice. Keep in mind, however, that some employment agencies charge a fee for their services, whereas most of the other sources listed in this chapter are free of charge. Employment agencies are almost always listed in the yellow pages under "Employment." You might also want to consider talking with a temporary employment agency. Many such agencies often help people find long-term, full-time employment, and temporary situations often turn into permanent ones.

JOB APPLICATION PROCEDURES

Different jobs require different application procedures. The rule of thumb is to follow all application guidelines strictly. If an employer states in an advertisement for a position that résumés should be sent and that no phone calls will be accepted, then you should send your résumé (along with a cover letter, of course) and not call the company. Although following such a simple direction may seem like common sense, I've had many clients tell me that they always thought it would be a good idea to call the company anyway—even though the advertisement for the position said only to "send a resume." Think about it for a moment: If you were an employer, would you want to hire someone who followed directions or not?

Most jobs require prospective employees to complete an application form. If you have the opportunity to complete an application at home, then by all means do so. If you have access to a typewriter, the application should definitely be typed. If you don't have a typewriter available to you, then at least *very neatly* print all of your information. If you must complete the application on site, then you should use a ball-point pen (blue or black ink) unless otherwise directed. Be sure to take your time to complete the information neatly and accurately. It's also a good idea to dress appropriately when completing an application on site, even if a job interview won't be conducted at that time. The first impression you make is often a lasting one.

Be sure you have all of the necessary information with you in case you have to complete applications on site. Information that is routinely requested on job applications is outlined below.

JOB APPLICATION INFORMATION

YOUR NAME, CURRENT ADDRESS, AND TELEPHONE NUMBER

Many applications will also ask you to provide information (at least the address and telephone number) of your current employment site, so be sure to have that information handy as well. You might also be asked to list your previous home address and phone number—especially if you've been living at your current residence for less than two years.

EDUCATIONAL BACKGROUND

Most applications require you to list high school and college information, including names, addresses, and telephone numbers of the institutions you attended. You'll also probably be asked to indicate how many hours of course work you've completed at each educational level and what type of diploma, degree, or certificate was awarded to you. Dates of graduation and/or certification will be requested on most applications.

PREVIOUS WORK EXPERIENCES

Even if you have a résumé available, many employers will still want you to list your previous work experiences on the application. You'll need to have the starting and ending dates of your previous employment, the names and addresses of the companies or organizations you worked for, the names and phone numbers of your immediate supervisors, and a brief description of the work-related responsibilities associated with each job. You may also be asked to provide information about your salary history. Applications often require you to list both your starting and ending pay for each of your previous jobs.

PERSONAL AND PROFESSIONAL REFERENCES

Most applications also ask for contact information (names, addresses, and phone numbers) for both personal and professional references. Personal references are those people you would consider friends. The personal references you list on a job application should be people who know you quite well on an interpersonal level: people you've known for at least a year or two. Professional references can include former supervisors, teachers, or even coworkers who can attest to the quality of your work. Make sure you have all of the contact information for at least four or five personal and four or five professional references just to be safe.

MISCELLANEOUS INFORMATION

Depending on the application, you might be asked to provide a variety of additional information, ranging from a list of your hobbies and interests to previous awards you've received and special talents and skills you have. Taking along a copy of your résumé when completing an application on site would surely come in handy. But you should probably also take a folder with you—one that contains this additional information you may need.

THE EMPLOYMENT INTERVIEW

My first suggestion regarding job interviews is that you attend a workshop on job interviewing skills. Most career centers offer interviewing skills workshops that can be especially effective for individuals who don't have a whole lot of interviewing experience. Some of these workshops even provide a videotaping service, in which a mock interview is taped so that you can see how you interact with someone during an interview situation. If you're unable to attend an interview skills workshop, then practice with a friend or family member. After running through a few "trials," you'll be much more prepared for an actual interview.

Another important point to consider is *always* to dress as professionally as possible when interviewing for a job—even for jobs that don't require strict dress codes. As mentioned before, that first impression you'll make is going to last a long time. When hundreds of people are applying for a few job openings, everything that you say and do plays an important role in whether or not you get the job.

It's also a good idea to go to an interview well prepared. Researching the company, for example, can give you a sense of what direction the company is moving in. This might help you anticipate the kinds of questions that you'll be asked during the interview. It also helps you come up with something interesting and meaningful to say when the interviewer asks you if *you* have any questions about the company or the position.

Make sure you will be able to find the location of the interview prior to the actual day of your appointment. The last thing you want to do on your way to an interview is get lost. By finding out where you're interview is going to be held in advance, you'll also decrease some of the anxiety that is a natural part of interviewing for a job.

The following box summarizes ways that you can best prepare for a job interview.

Summary of Important Tips for Job Interview Preparation

- Attend job interview workshops
- Practice interview skills with a friend
- Dress professionally (no matter what type of job it is)
- Find out more about the company through research
- Anticipate the questions you'll be asked and prepare answers accordingly
- Be prepared to ask questions of the interviewer
- Find out how to get to the interview location in advance

Preparation is the key to successful job search strategies and application procedures. Even if it'll be several months or even years before you'll be applying for a job, now is the time to prepare. If you haven't already started, begin learning *now* how you can go about finding job opportunities in the career you're pursuing. Put together a résumé *today*—before you find yourself in the need of developing one at the last minute. Collect all of the information you're likely to need to complete a job application and keep it organized in a file, updating it as necessary. Attend job interview workshops *whenever they're offered,* and seek one-on-one assistance from a career counselor if you think that it'll help. The key is to be prepared for what lies ahead. Exactly how prepared you're going to be when the time comes to obtain a job is up to only one person . . . and that person is *you!*

Job Satisfaction Questionnaire

Whether now or at some point in the future, you may want to evaluate a particular occupation or career choice. By completing a job satisfaction questionnaire, you'll be able to identify those aspects of your current job that are rewarding as well as those that contribute to dissatisfaction. The results will help you clarify the aspects of a job that most directly contribute to your career satisfaction. You can also use this exercise to predict how you *might* respond to *potential* occupations and the degree of satisfaction that a potential job is likely to provide.

PART I

GENERAL INFORMATION

Occupation: _____

How long have you worked for this company? _____

What previous positions have you held with the company? _____

_____

_____

What is your job title? _____

How long have you held your current position? _____

Briefly describe your work responsibilities (as you would on a résumé):

_____

_____

_____

_____

_____

PART II

RATING YOUR CURRENT JOB SATISFACTION

1	2	3	4	5
not satisfied at all		somewhat satisfied		extremely satisfied

Using the scale shown above, rate your level of satisfaction with the following aspects of your job.

GENERAL WORKING CONDITIONS

_____ Hours Worked Each Week

_____ Flexibility in Scheduling

_____ Location of Work

_____ Amount of Paid Vacation Time/Sick Leave Offered

PAY AND PROMOTION POTENTIAL

_____ Salary

_____ Opportunities for Promotion

_____ Benefits (Health Insurance, Life Insurance, etc.)

_____ Job Security

_____ Recognition for Work Accomplished

WORK RELATIONSHIPS

_____ Relationships With Your Co-workers

_____ Relationship(s) With Your Supervisor(s)

_____ Relationships With Your Subordinates (if applicable)

USE OF SKILLS AND ABILITIES

_____ Opportunity to Utilize Your Skills and Talents

_____ Opportunity to Learn New Skills

_____ Support for Additional Training and Education

WORK ACTIVITIES

_____ Variety of Job Responsibilities

_____ Degree of Independence Associated With Your Work Roles

_____ Adequate Opportunity for Periodic Changes in Duties

OTHER ASPECTS OF THE JOB RELATING TO YOUR LEVEL OF SATISFACTION

Review your ratings. List the items below for which your satisfaction level was a 4 or a 5:

_____

_____

_____

_____

_____

_____

_____

_____

These are the aspects of your current job with which you are generally satisfied. As you consider potential career changes in the future, make sure you take into account those things about your current job that are satisfying.

Now list the items below for which your satisfaction level was a 1 or a 2.

_____

_____

_____

_____

_____

These are the characteristics associated with your current work situation that are dissatisfying. These aspects of your job are the types of things that you'll want to avoid in any future career or occupational choice. You can gain a better understanding of what to look for in a future career change by analyzing what it is that you dislike about your current job.

As you consider changing your career plans, whether now or at some point in the future, try to make the types of changes that'll lead to an increase in your overall job satisfaction.

Bibliography

Bandura, A. (1977). Self-efficacy: Toward a unifying theory of behavioral change. *Psychological Review* 84, 191–215.

Bandura, A. (1982). Self-efficacy mechanism in human agency. *American Psychologist* 37, 122–147.

Bandura, A. (1986). *Social foundations of thought and action: A social cognitive theory.* Englewood Cliffs, NJ: Prentice Hall.

Campbell, D. P. (1992). *Campbell Interest and Skills Survey.* Minneapolis MN: NCS Assessments.

Career Development Quarterly. (Published four times each year). Alexandria, VA: National Career Development Association.

Encyclopedia of careers and vocational guidance. (1990). Chicago: J. G. Ferguson.

Hammer, A. L. *Introduction to type and careers.* Palo Alto, CA: Consulting Psychologists Press.

Holland, J. L. (1985). *Making vocational choices: A theory of vocational personalities and work environments* (2nd ed). Englewood Cliffs, NJ: Prentice Hall.

Holland, J. L. (1996). *Self-Directed Search.* Odessa, FL: Psychological Assessment Resources.

Kapes, J. T., M. M. Mastie, and E. A. Whitfield. (1994). *A counselor's guide to career assessment instruments* (3rd ed.). Alexandria, VA: National Career Development Association.

Naisbitt, J., and P. Aburdene. (1990). *Megatrends 2000: Ten new directions for the 1990s.* New York: Avon.

Roe, A. (1956). *The psychology of occupations.* New York: Wiley & Sons.

Roe, A., and P. W. Lunneborg. (1984). Personality development and career choice. In D. Brown, L. Brooks, & Associates (Eds.), *Career choice and development,* (pp. 31–60). San Francisco: Jossey-Bass.

Strong Interest Inventory of the Strong Vocational Interest Blanks. Palo Alto, CA: Consulting Psychologists Press.

Super, D. E. (1990). A life-span, life-space approach to career development. In D. Brown, L. Brooks, & Associates (Eds.), *Career choice and development,* (2nd ed). San Francisco: Jossey-Bass.

Super, D. E., and D. D. Nevill. (1986). *The Values Scale.* Palo Alto, CA: Consulting Psychologists Press.

U. S. Department of Labor. (1991). *Guide to occupational exploration.* Washington, DC: U.S. Government Printing Office.

U. S. Department of Labor. (Updated Biannually). *Occupational Outlook Handbook.* Washington, DC: U.S. Government Printing Office.

U. S. Department of Labor. (Published four times a year). *Occupational Outlook Quarterly.* Washington, DC: U.S. Government Printing Office.

U. S. Department of Labor. (1990). *Opportunity 2000.* Washington, DC: U.S. Government Printing Office.

U. S. Employment Service. (1991). *Dictionary of occupational titles* (4th ed., revised). Washington, DC: U.S. Government Printing Office.

Witt, M. A. (1992). *Job strategies for people with disabilities.* Princeton, NJ: Peterson's Guides.

Index